A Treasury

of

Trueness

Previously unpublished
writings of
VERNON HOWARD

Compiled and published by
NEW LIFE FOUNDATION
Pine AZ 85544
(520) 476-3224

Selected works of
VERNON HOWARD
compiled and published by
New Life Foundation
under license.

First Printing 1995

ISBN 0-911203-33-8

New Life Foundation
PO Box 2230
Pine AZ 85544
(520) 476-3224

> "Just as there are millions
> of unseen stars,
> there are endless inner riches
> for you to discover."
>
> —Vernon Howard

4/7

Dear Kate

Here's' the roadmap
to our happiness — an
inside job

Love Jim dl,

Introduction

This compilation of higher knowledge and spiritual guidance provides practical steps by which you can learn all about yourself and all about other people. For any who will allow it to, Truth heals all of life's pains and stings. It will enable you to handle any crisis life can bring.

Here you will meet over 2,300 short, powerful truths that show you how to be truly happy and in command every moment. These practical spiritual principles collect the essence of life into one magnificent, concentrated volume you will want to draw on daily.

Vernon Howard, probably the clearest writer on higher living the world has ever known, shared priceless gems of wisdom with his students for over twenty years. The valuable nuggets of spiritual gold organized here do not appear in any of his other books or booklets. Every problem on earth is revealed and explained, whether it's about yourself or someone else. And the *Table of Contents* points you to instant help with any question that is troubling you.

We are limited by our present way of thinking. Vernon Howard teaches there *is* another way to live. A new life **can** be yours, one that's free from all pain and heartache. For there truly is something else beyond the human mind that can and will come to our rescue.

Men and women today long for real and lasting inner peace. They fail to realize how many difficulties show up because they just don't understand. They need the strong medicine that brings the healing influences of the stars to our doorstep.

There is a cosmic law that all true spiritual effort is rewarded. Every time you read and reflect on these beautiful truths, every time you put the spiritual exercises into practice, you guarantee that heaven receives notice of your interest. God *will* send you help.

The secrets contained in the pages of this treasury book will tell you solutions the world doesn't want you to know about. But the true purpose of life *is* known. God knows, and you can too. Get ready to enter upon the greatest adventure any man or woman could ever experience. Welcome these wonderful truths and they will become your very own. That's what it's all about!

Table of Contents *Page*

Chapter 1

THE POWER OF TRUENESS

YOUR TRUE PURPOSE IN LIFE

1. It is wise to seek immortality because time defeats all other ambitions.

2. The purpose of life is to let human life be replaced by spiritual life.

3. You have a spiritual birth certificate but you have misplaced it. It is the birth certificate of citizenship in the Higher Kingdom.

4. God is pure Truth. It is the only power that exists.

5. The purpose of life is to outgrow your dependence on physical places, people and things and develop within you a source of higher power.

6. God wants to live His life through you.

7. Discover who you really are—and change everything!

8. The purpose of life is to rise above yourself.

9. Nothing is important in life except to be spiritually awake right now.

10. Your real purpose must be to reunite with God.

11. Negative states want to keep you from discovering the purpose of your life. And the purpose of your life is to find something stronger than this life.

12. Your first duty is toward yourself, your inner freedom, the Truth.

TRUTH IS OUR ONLY FRIEND

13. Truth is the only thing that, every time you make contact with it, you feel good.

14. Truth is simply what remains after human delusion has been removed through self-insight.

15. The Truth is for those who no longer want to suffer.

16. What the world has done to you, Truth can undo.

17. Truth does not hurt. Rather, it is our resistance to its message that causes pain.

18. The rules of Truth are your friends. They are enemies to what is your enemy.

19. There are higher things to think about.

20. Something exists in the universe other than your mind.

21. The supreme wonder of the world is that Truth exists.

DISCOVER THE NEED FOR SOMETHING ELSE

22. There is only good in telling yourself the Truth.

23. You know that you are not living from the right place within. You *know* that.

24. Life is for realizing that there is something else besides the way we have usually, normally lived.

25. Deep down inside, you want two things: something valuable and something everlasting.

26. Feel the need for something different, then let it grow by having affection for it.

27. You will never, never be disappointed at what happens to you as a result of your wanting to transcend yourself. The reason for this is that there is a compassionate force that exists which understands

you and recognizes even the smallest portion of higher desire in you and immediately races to your rescue.

SETTING RIGHT GOALS

28. In your spiritual life you must have a noble aim.

29. Sooner or later you will have to decide whether to write a movie script about your life or write a true story.

30. The great goal of life is to get up knowing that you are going to wake up.

31. The noble aim supplies the practical how.

32. You can no longer believe in your own self-written propaganda about yourself? Congratulations. You are on the way.

33. The most noble thing on earth is the man or woman who truly aspires to the higher life and is making all the sincere efforts he or she can to arrive there.

BECOME A GOOD SPIRITUAL STUDENT

34. Spiritual growth cannot happen without a very, very special effort of going against life.

35. Always walk through life as if you have something new to learn and you will.

36. Do not let a day go by without snapping the mind's mechanicalness to become conscious and aware. Ask, "What thought just passed through my mind?" Be aware of the thought, then let it go. That is all, but it has deep power.

37. Make an effort to simplify your work on yourself. Use simple words. If you have hatred, use the word *hatred* not *a mild resentment*. Don't use nice words to complicate the task. Use the words that hurt. That shows you what you are really like.

38. Self-knowledge creates an inner state in which you are valuable to yourself in a new way.

39. The nice thing about inner work is that it does not connect with any opposite conditions. This means you are free to work when irritated or untroubled, when alone or with others, when speaking or listening. The river flows with equal ease during both night and noon toward its desired destination.

40. Never fear to study human evil, just as you would study science or geography.

41. People are afraid to study Satan because they're afraid that it will lead back to themselves.

42. There is work to do. Do the work.

43. You must both know and feel that you have much work to do on yourself. It is this combination that produces the necessary energy for the work.

44. The book of life must be read one hundred percent. You must be a diligent student.

45. Right and constant inner work is all that matters. Inner work is the whole and only answer to everything.

46. Be in the classroom twenty-four hours a day.

47. There is always so much more to learn.

48. Learn to love learning. Collecting knowledge can be one of life's most enjoyable pursuits. You can educate yourself right into the Kingdom of Heaven.

49. When faced with your task of being a mechanic or schoolteacher or doctor you may be very competent, but what happens when you are faced with being a human being?

50. A man grows up, collects vast amounts of facts and takes this collection of facts as himself. Then he makes a monumental mistake. He says, *"I* must survive."

51. Your day is filled with strain and pain because of a certain unseen and frantic activity. You try to prove that you can leap over the tall wall and preferably ahead of everyone else. Do you know that there is really neither a wall nor a leaper?

52. All the grief on earth can be traced back to this cause: Having nothing truly worthwhile in his life, a man creates false values, false goals, false activities.

53. One hundred times a day an individual tries painfully to convince himself that his various actions are important, sensible, beneficial, necessary. This means that every day he commits one hundred crimes against himself.

WE GET BACK WHAT WE GIVE OUT

54. All day long we attract the same things we send out.

55. Your nature and your experiences are one. Your conditions and experiences are one.

56. The level of your actions decides the level of your results in life. You get what you give and you get what you are.

57. When you send a mean remark, look or attitude toward someone, it happens because you are

asleep. You are your own worst enemy and don't even know it because you have no right values.

58. You always meet yourself wherever you go.

59. Because you are nervous, everyone and everything responds to you with nervousness.

60. How clearly do you understand the spiritual law that if you hurt someone else, you hurt yourself?

61. As long as you're in a state of psychological desire, you'll attract the same low level to yourself.

62. We attract events which correspond to our nature, so a higher nature will attract higher events.

IMPORTANT FACTS TO REMEMBER

63. Happiness is better than misery.

64. We suffer only from unlearned lessons.

65. Personal happiness depends on the number of higher laws you obey. Personal anguish depends on the number of higher laws you disobey.

66. There is nothing to gain. There's something to give up.

67. Something inside you is deceiving you. It is working full time to prevent you from discovering this.

68. No human being knowingly injures himself.

69. There is no self to be happy, there is only happiness.

70. Nothing is more practical than these studies.

HIGHER TRUTHS CAN BE UNDERSTOOD

71. There is no excuse for an inability to understand higher truths, for if you cancel refusal to understand, you cancel inability to understand.

72. Inner guidance is heard like soft music in the night by those who have learned to listen.

73. No one ever learns from experience alone. To the experience must be added the powers of watchfulness, perception, information, detachment and a strong wish to not be deceived by the experience. For example, when someone tries to take advantage of you, that is the experience. But to learn from it, you must not return your deceit for his deceit; your motives must be different from his. Your higher nature then releases and connects you with lesson-learning powers.

74. Learning means leaving yourself.

75. You can either think about yourself or you can study yourself. The difference between the two is the difference between chains and liberty.

THE VALUE OF A CLEAR MIND

76. Think of the beauty of the word *clear*.

77. All you need is a clear mind and spirit.

78. How terrible not to be able to see a challenge with a clear mind and not make a problem out of it.

79. You fear clarity because in a clear mind there is no *you*.

80. The feeling of being in danger from oneself fades with the application of higher facts.

81. Deception in any man or woman can never hide from clear thinking. So take one deception a day and look for it in a particular human being and then in yourself.

82. Always value a clear mind. It is the doorway to the Higher World.

83. Prayer: "God, please make everything clear to me."

QUESTION YOUR PRESENT WAY OF THINKING

84. You really think that something out there hurts you, not knowing that you are your own hurt.

85. There is a way to think toward a surrounding threat that is stronger than the threat. There is a way to think toward a loss that is stronger than the loss.

86. Watch and see whether that arising thought causes you pain or regret. Know that it is an unnecessary thought. At first it is hard to see that it is unnecessary because thought itself will lie to you and insist that your life depends upon the presence of painful thoughts. Your nervous life does indeed depend upon tormenting thoughts of all kinds, but that is not the kind of a life you want.

87. You're afraid that your runaway mind will not come to a stop. And you're afraid that it will. See the contradiction you live in at every turn!

88. Divided energy produces conflict.

89. Question the value of letting this jackrabbit mind have its way.

90. There is a simple method by which anyone can triple his energy and efficiency. Just realize that it is unnecessary to think nine out of ten thoughts you now think.

91. The life of a losing human being is dominated by repetitious and blundering thoughts. The life of a winning human being is dominated by new and revealing light.

BELIEF CAUSES GRIEF

92. Acquired beliefs and cosmic facts are as different as pebbles and diamonds.

93. The human mind is a phonograph record and we believe in it.

94. Anything you wish to believe is false.

95. Thinking that stubborn beliefs can give us a new life is like watching a stone statue, hoping it will move.

96. Confined beliefs cannot create a spacious life.

97. The vanishing of belief invites the appearance of Pure Energy that lives your life for you. Nothing is nicer than to not live your own life based on belief. Your own life derived from Pure Energy is pleasant, lighthearted, carefree.

WE MUST SEE OURSELVES AS WE ARE

98. If once a day you told yourself what kind of person you really are, something new would begin to happen to you.

99. When I spill food all over the floor my reaction is what I really am.

100. You can be appalled at what you've been without being self-critical over it.

101. Vernon, I finally understand what you mean by conscious indifference to daily events. I no longer care what happens as long as it happens to someone else.

102. You have a dull ache and you don't know what to do about it.

103. You must see where you are consenting to your own torment.

104. You feel obligated to feel discomfort and ill-at-ease.

105. Incredibly, darkness has convinced you that you need sickness in order to be happy.

106. The problem is not that you are captive, for you can get out of any problem you're in. The problem is that you don't see that you are captive.

107. You have it all planned out, don't you? And the next day you have to plan it out again.

108. Only by seeing that your life is not important as it now unfolds can you finally see how rightly important it can be. This new and true feeling of importance will not be given to you by yourself, but by something that is not yourself.

109. You become eligible for the higher by clearly seeing your yearning for the lower.

THE BLUNT AND THE BEAUTIFUL

110. There is such a thing as the radiation of rightness. And guess who enjoys the radiations first? You!

111. The purpose of this class is not to scare anyone, as most newcomers think, but to forever scare the scares away.

112. Do you ever have any kind of a fear of what your own neurosis might get you into—the trouble that you might get yourself into? It's all because you can't judge between right and wrong, between what is authentically good for you and what you assume is good for you.

113. You invent the fear, the obstacle, the threat, because you would rather vibrate with fear than find eternal life.

114. I have marvelous, wonderful news. Listen carefully and feel the surge of relief that will pass through you. Here it is: You need no longer pretend that you understand yourself and life.

115. Here is one question you can ask a person that determines whether or not he has a chance to be different. That question is, "Are you a confused human being?" If he answers yes from his heart, he has a chance. If he lies and says no, or if he answers yes while thinking no, he has no chance at all.

116. We are here in class to be as foolish as we really are, and there is nothing foolish about that.

117. Truth is the only thing that can put the blunt and the beautiful together rightly.

118. The Truth is tough because it's tender.

119. The Truth in this class radiates out and touches that man in Europe, the lady in Canada. It reaches that one person in 500,000 who has been looking for this all their lives.

FACTS ABOUT HUMAN NATURE

120. The entire human problem resides in a peculiarity of human nature—its unwillingness to explore human nature.

121. Talking to the average man about something higher than sex and money is like talking to a rabbit about a rainbow.

122. The right thing to talk about is the loss of self-glorification.

123. Human beings almost always prefer familiar errors over unknown truths.

124. If you really understand human nature, you also understand how and why everything happens on earth.

125. You will understand human badness better by

seeing its cause in deep, haunting and unadmitted insecurity.

126. Insecurity snarls.

127. People want to be in control of events and people instead of themselves.

128. Two weak people always hate each other, for the weakness in one reminds the other one of his own weakness.

129. Desperation has no consideration.

130. Most men have a character that is only one inch deep. Under that is a storehouse of fireworks.

131. Everyone is nothing but a collection of wild ideas. See them this way. See everyone you meet as a collection of wild ideas.

132. Peace is the enemy of human beings. They will do anything to destroy peace.

133. Human beings always treat you the way they treat themselves.

134. The human cannot cure the human.

135. The more you learn about human nature, the more you are attracted to divine nature.

TAKE YOUR LIFE BACK

136. You have your friends and your finances, you have your activities and your tomorrows. How pathetic that you have everything but your own life.

137. Presently you can't live your own life because you don't know what it means to live your own life. What it means to live your own life is to no longer live from the belief that you are living your own life.

138. The old nature prays for nothing but its own repetition.

139. When you feel the temptation to be nervous, flustered, bumbly, turn to your own shaking and weakness and say, "I'm not living for you anymore."

140. To start life over means you have to abandon every single plan you have psychologically, not businesswise or for building the house or things like that, but psychologically, mentally, spiritually. Abandon all hope ye who enter the Temple of Truth. You must, otherwise you will stay on the shaky, trembling level of ordinary thought and scheme ways to make yourself happy, to start life afresh and leave the problems behind. If you really want to start life fresh, just know that *you* can't start life all over, for *you* are the past. Instead, know that there's no one there who has to start a new life. When *you* vanish, that is the new life.

141. Be aware of how people insist upon draining your energy, then quietly refuse it.

142. Your morning prayer: This is the beginning of a new day. This is the beginning of a new life.

DANGEROUS DAYDREAMS

143. Imagination is a place of pain. See it. As long as imagination is operating, Truth can't. See the results of what you're doing, how it all does nothing for you. Imagination says that if you think about something, it will come to you. Not so. You're believing in a magic wand from reading too many stories in childish books. You wave your wand all day long, but nothing happens. Throw out one false dream a day. That would be super progress.

144. Dreamland is screamland.

145. You are not living where your colorful fantasies say you are. But you can't see that you are living in fairy tales authored by your own nervous imagination. And to complete your mental illness, you reject rescuing realities as fairy tales.

146. Imagination is a false and evil magician.

147. The enemy is unseen self-starring daydreams. Work at catching your daydreams as they start to form.

148. Imagination is an incredibly persistent enemy.

149. Few things are more dangerous than to have an image of being an independent person: "Nobody tells me what to do!" *Everybody* tells that man what to do.

150. You are weak because you have pictures of being strong.

151. All evil, all sinfulness, all wickedness is a state of not knowing yourself as you really are. Therefore, you behave, or I behave, mechanically. And I destroy me and you with this same psychic sleep that I have in myself.

152. Mental and spiritual health is the lack of self-images.

SNAP THE SPELL

153. Don't fight Reality when it penetrates your dream world.

154. I don't care what you have brought upon yourself, one refusal to run the film and it is just as if it never existed.

155. Outwit your own neurosis. Stop being in love with being mad! Do you know how much energy is wasted in running favorite mad mental movies?

156. When you drop a thought the moment it appears, you prevent it from forming a false "I." That is, you prevent harmful identification. So thought cannot cluster to form damaging self-images of being *wise* or *secure* or *loved.*

157. To wake up means to no longer unknowingly toss coals onto your uncomfortable inner fire.

158. You can't wake up until you know you're asleep.

159. When you're awake you feel good. When you're asleep you feel bad. There is great power in this simple statement.

FREEDOM FROM FEAR

160. Fear disperses natural powers of growth and protection.

161. Fear fiercely refuses to let you investigate itself, so the only cheerful thing for you to do is investigate it.

162. You won't look at what you're afraid of for fear it will make you afraid.

163. Since you're already in fear, you have nothing more to fear by exploring fear.

164. Simple understanding has no fears.

165. Fear presents itself as the solution to your fear.

166. In the true world fear doesn't exist.

167. Fear is the time-self, but not the eternal self.

168. Your true self cannot be afraid of anyone.

STOP IT!

169. Refuse to pass along the box of badness that was passed on to you.

170. Remind yourself daily, "Isn't there enough pain in the world already without me adding to it?"

171. The other person has a right to his own life and you have no right to demand that he give it to your neurosis.

172. No, I'm not going along with you this time!

173. When you walk into a room from now on say, "I don't want to hurt a single person in this room in the slightest way possible."

174. The state of feeling intimidated blocks your awareness of what is going on, so it is necessary to observe this. Someone you are afraid of makes a minor contemptuous remark and you don't even notice it. You grin weakly. Stop that defensive weak smile when people make cutting remarks to you. Keep that face of yours straight. Look them right in the eye and send them a message like, "Knock it off!"

HELP FROM TRUTH

175. The only person who can really take care of you is a person who knows how to take care of himself. With this fact in mind, how many people do you know who can take care of you?

176. A spiritual teacher is anyone who gives to others by his word or his manner the spiritual treasures which were originally given to him.

177. The only person who really understands goodness is someone who really understands evil.

178. Phony gentleness destroys.

179. A teacher must put every inquirer in a position where the inquirer can no longer get away with his usual lies and evils. In this small corner, the inquirer will

always reveal himself as he really is—as either a phony who should be promptly dismissed or as someone who really wishes to become a spiritual student.

180. There is a powerful cry in a weak person when in contact with a strong person. The weak individual silently cries out, "Please don't tell me that I am all right when I am really all wrong. Don't let me get away with my sick behavior. Even if I hate you for rebuking me, please keep telling me how foolish I am. Please be stronger than my hatred, for I am not. Deep within I know that your strength is the only chance I have."

181. One thing that you don't see is that you are seen through. Wrongly taking yourself as being real, you foolishly assume that spiritual wisdom is under the same delusion. This leaves you helpless. So you must remember that only someone who sees through you can help you. But you must let the Higher help you. It will pain your vanity but the pain will finally pass. The sooner you submit to the lesson, the sooner you will nicely feel right about yourself.

182. The Truth is seeping through your resistance. It is working. I feel it!

183. A real teacher has a lighted lantern in each hand. He first motions with one hand for the inquirer to go away. The wise inquirer is one who stands in place after the apparent rejection just to see what happens next. And what happens next is the teacher's second motion from the other lantern, which is an invitation to approach. When accepting the invitation, the inquirer is surprised and pleased to find himself within the single circle of light from both lanterns.

STOP SINKING WITH THINKING

184. You cannot solve your problem by thinking about yourself.

185. Suffering always runs along the track of mechanical thought, so by permitting consciousness to interrupt mechanical thought, we learn the secret for ending suffering.

186. Investigate your own mind from second to second. See the nature of this mind. Nothing matters except what "I" want.

187. Unnecessary thinking blocks right action.

188. Something that may be extremely important to frantic thought has no value whatever to higher insight.

189. Disorders are healed when lifted to a higher plane of thought than the plane which caused them, for on this higher plane we cease to interfere with the healing.

190. A jolt must precede growth, a jolt being where you knock a mechanical thought off the track.

191. Consulting one wild thought after another will keep you wild.

ESCAPE THE PRISON OF SELF

192. Every person is either his own enjoyable castle or his very sad prison.

193. The first few years of life we build a brick wall around us.

194. In the prison is the belief that you must create a heaven. Trying to create a heaven in the dungeon is frustrating.

195. You will never get out of prison until you know absolutely that it is the wrong place for you to be.

196. All attempts of the prison-self to get out of prison are part of the prison.

197. One of the last barriers to fall is the pretense of knowing what one really knows nothing about. Pretense is one of the strongest cronies of self-sickness.

198. The prison is an illusion.

199. Walk out! There are no barriers. Only your wish to stay in the prison camp keeps you there.

200. Every spiritual step must be accompanied by the willingness and the appearance of feeling foolish. There is no escape from the prison of your old acquired self without a deliberate, consistent willingness to appear foolish before yourself and others. The willingness to appear foolish causes great, beautiful destruction. The only question that is left is this: "How fast can I go? How ingenious can I be in inventing ways to be foolish before you and myself?" You know that the reason we want to appear wise before others is because we want a picture of ourselves presented to them. Now we are going to do the exact opposite of everything we used to do.

201. God wants to break through. He wants to shatter the wall and give you the entire kingdom.

SELF-HONESTY

202. Work for self-honesty. With that God can do the rest. Without it God can do nothing for you.

203. Say, "Truth, I want to know what is right. Please inform me what is truly best for me."

204. You think it is easy to be honest? No, it is the most difficult thing on earth to be honest. It is the last thing human beings want to do. Say to yourself right now, "I am a lost human being." Now, that is honesty.

205. Honesty feels good. Lies feel bad.

206. Self-honesty coupled with self-investigation will bring you to self-healing.

207. You can fall out of love with your false nature if you are honest enough to examine what it has given you.

208. Every single effort is rewarded. It may not come immediately, but it always comes.

209. Self-honesty is a million times more powerful and healing than you know.

TRUE ENCOURAGEMENT

210. True encouragement occurs when you hear a truth you already knew faintly.

211. Real progress is when you learn something you thought you knew all along.

212. No one is more qualified than you to discover the true treasures of your inner kingdom.

213. No one who hears the Truth can ever forget it.

214. Facts—no matter how frightening they seem to be—are always on your side.

215. Remember, there is nothing wrong about something being true.

216. Simply put yourself in a position to be helped.

217. Instead of blaming the outer world, examine the inner world.

218. Thought must be obedient to Spirit.

219. I'm not me anymore!

220. Whether felt or not, healing always follows deliberate suffering of any kind.

221. You will be at work some day or around the house and suddenly something will enter you and comfort you. It is coming from the Higher World.

222. The greatest day in your life is when you hear the voice of God.

INNER-WORK EXERCISES

THE LIGHT SWITCH Whenever you turn a light switch on or off, know that you're doing it. You may be quite amused to see that you can't do it all the time. Isn't awareness of unawareness actually awareness?

RELAX AND REALIZE Sit or lie relaxed and watch what is going on in your mind. Whatever you think—that is what you are at that moment. You will see there is no controller, just vagabond thoughts.

TO CLEAR YOUR MIND To clear your mind, ask yourself, "How can I say this in the simplest, shortest and best way instead of complicating it?"

OUCH, BUT THAT'S RIGHT Write down, "Ouch, but that's right," on a piece of paper, followed by "Do nothing with mental pain." Then underneath add several things you usually do with your pain— fight it, resent it, etc. When you do anything with your mental pain, you are adding you to it. Leave the *"ouch"* alone and it will go away; otherwise, you'll be an *ouch-grouch*. Your weaknesses will now collaborate to find ways you can do something with the pain. However, Light is always stronger than darkness. Do this exercise for three days on three separate pieces of paper and do not look at the papers until the fourth day. The written words will be imprinted inwardly where they can work on you automatically.

• • •

Chapter 2
HOW TO BE TRULY HAPPY

UNDERSTANDING IS THE KEY

223. What I'm about to tell you is so important, please write it down: Seek insight, not happiness.

224. All can be well because all can be understood.

225. Everything necessary to true happiness can be obtained. It is essential to learn to distinguish between the necessary and the unnecessary.

226. The truly necessary and vital thing is to realize we are here on earth to rise above ourselves.

227. Cosmic wisdom reveals why unhappy events happen, after which they cease to happen.

228. Happiness consists of knowing the answer to the question, "Who is this defeat happening to?" The answer is, "No one."

229. Understanding of your present nature is the answer.

230. Spiritual Knowing is Spiritual Glowing. It is a pleasant feeling, a released intelligence that shines naturally on anything.

ASK YOURSELF

231. How would you like to take a vacation from yourself? Wouldn't that be the delight of your life?

232. Do you understand that you're supposed to enjoy your life on earth?

233. A self-question: What has not happened to me yet that will cast me into gloom when it does?

234. Who are you trying to make happy?

235. If everyone in the world went around like you, what kind of a world would it be?

236. Why does my song always go wrong?

237. God doesn't require you to suffer. Why are you requiring it?

238. Where are you creating an activity in order not to see how empty you are?

239. To be in your company—a pleasure or a pain?

240. Ask yourself, "Am I pleasant to myself right now?"

241. Whatever way you now live is the way you insist is the best way and the safe way for you to live. And you keep saying to yourself that your present way is the best way and the safe way for you to live. Are you not curious as to why you must keep saying that to yourself?

242. Resistance to the disturbance is the disturbance, so why resist?

243. Isn't it strange that we must get used to being happy?

244. Don't you want to know more?

245. Do you want to please others or the Truth within?

246. Always ask yourself these questions: "Is it true? Is it kind? Is it necessary?"

WHAT IF?

247. Examining the doubts we have about our present way is a highly intelligent act.

248. There are three stages that a person on the path passes through: 1. I know what I want. 2. I don't know what I want. 3. I really know what I want.

249. A billion times you have sought your own answers. Do you want to go into the second billion?

250. Think seriously about your life condition, not sadly.

251. When admitting, "I just don't know the answer," you are doing something far more profound than you think. You place yourself at the foot of the stairs that lead upward to a world far higher than the intellect. When saying, "I just don't know the answer, you are coming to the end of the self-conceit and self-deceit that occupies the level of the intellect. You have qualified yourself for leaving the self-centered world and approaching the lofty universal world.

WE'RE LOOKING IN THE WRONG PLACES

252. You have built up a series of escapes to prevent yourself from finding happiness.

253. In his childishness a man looks for exciting surprises instead of healing revelations.

254. Human beings are interested in primarily three things: personalities, position and possessions.

255. No matter how stupid the activity, self-interest always calls it intelligent.

256. Human beings live in three stages of experience: Demand, Rejection, Frustration.

257. Few people ever really realize the following fact: Insecurity is a mental condition, not a condition of finances, friendships or sex. The few who do realize this can start the interesting journey that ends beyond ordinary mental conditions, where true security resides.

258. Happiness is when what is right and what interests you are the same thing.

THE ONLY THING YOU NEED

259. There are two ways you can go through life and only two: with foggy desire or Spiritual Insight.

260. Nothing visible can satisfy the invisible.

261. Human beings are sight slaves.

262. If you don't stop angrily demanding what you want, you will be punished. You will be punished by getting it.

263. Your wants are your haunts.

264. The fulfillment of desire is as big a frustration as its thwarting.

265. You change your wants by first seeing what your wants presently give you.

266. Your desire can never understand another person's opposing desire. Your desire's attitude toward another person's opposite desire will be one of hostility or confusion or tears. This means you are painfully chained to the other person's desire. Only your non-desire can understand the other person's desire and be peacefully free of it.

267. You must always get what you want because you always are what you want. You and your wants are one. To obtain higher things, obtain a higher nature, for they too are one.

268. You need only one thing—Spiritual Wisdom. See how that knocks away the 1,000 useless things you think you need?

CANCEL PAST MISTAKES

269. What would you give for an eraser that would wipe away all the painful memories of childhood, marriage, children and jobs? What would you give? You can have it.

270. Wrong action in the past is corrected perfectly by right action in the present.

271. You can cancel everything in the past if you cancel yourself.

272. All you have to do is give your willingness to let the Truth flow through you.

273. By working with yourself and with truthful ideas, you will one day silently say the following to another person: "Yes, I cruelly hurt you for a long time, and I finally see why. I hurt you because it was the only thing I knew to do. My own agony and confusion caused me to strike out at you in a vain attempt to relieve my own painful pressure. I knew of no other way to try to get rid of my own awful hurt. Now I really understand why I hurt you and in this new insight, I am truly sorry. I am truly sorry for the first time. I also know that I will never hurt you again. It will not happen again because I am no longer asleep while dreaming that I am awake."

274. Everything in your past can be magically changed into freedom and innocence. It is done by disconnecting your beliefs in yourself from your memories about the past. And this is done by abandoning your delusion that you own a separate personality.

HAPPINESS CANNOT EXIST IN TIME-THINKING

275. Happiness cannot have a cause except spiritual health, which includes mental health. Any other cause you discover is simply a new way to be unhappy.

276. You have dozens, hundreds of ideas about the kind of a person you are. These ideas have no relation to Reality at all. This is why you have problems. This is why you have anxieties. This is why you

have fears. This is why you feel left out when some-one else has more than you have. This is why you say unconsciously to others, "You have no business treating me that way." All thought connects with memory. All thought connects with time, with yesterday. To be free of everything—not 99%, but 100%—you have to be free of acquired thought.

277. Thinking creates time.

278. Remember that horrible thing that you did to that man, that woman—remember that? See, this is the you that is still alive because you haven't cut yourself off from the time-self by which you now presently identify yourself.

279. Time-thinking imposes its own false meaning onto life, injuring the time-thinker.

280. The habitual mind cannot know of the existence of the alternative to the habitual mind.

281. Someday you will know what it means to die instantly to thought. You will have no time-identity at all.

282. Heaven is the nonexistence of the thought-self.

283. Always remember that the Spiritual World has com-plete power and authority over all the thoughts of the lower world.

284. The more enthusiasm you have for your thought-created self, the less enthusiasm you have for life. The less enthusiasm you have for your thought-created self, the more enthusiasm you have for life.

STOP TRYING TO SOLVE YOUR PROBLEMS

285. Think of how different your life would be if you did not grab hold of the problems that come your way.

286. You need not make a problem out of a problem.

287. Since you and your problems are one, your problems are just as unreal as you are.

288. You can't solve problems one at a time. You solve all problems or keep all.

289. When you have any kind of difficulty of any degree at all, why don't you not try to solve it? Just let it go. It will keep coming back. Why don't you give up the compulsive need to have an opinion about the problem? Track it back and find out who is frantic over solving the problem. The frantic self wants its answer. You say to yourself, "If only that person who is obstructing what I want will get out of the way, that will solve the problem." What if I don't create the problem in the first place by creating who I am? There is not a thing you can do about solving the problem. All you can do is cease to be the problem-creator, which means the absence of *me*. Then there is a totally different kind of self.

290. Most people merely rearrange their problems, but with self-insight you can end them.

291. You can't make problems disappear, but you can disappear to problems.

STUDY SUFFERING

292. Be a mind scientist.

293. A mature mind sees long-distance cause and effect. An immature mind sees only instant ego-gratification, regardless of the consequences.

294. If you are what you think about all day long, what are you?

295. Here is the difference between mental sickness and spiritual health: Mental sickness dramatizes human suffering, which makes it incapable of offering the cure. Spiritual health understands human suffering, which qualifies it to present the cure.

296. Every person who suffers, deep down senses he is the cause of it.

297. The reason you suffer is because you haven't gone thoroughly into suffering to come out on the other side.

298. The state you are suffering is telling you all about itself.

299. You could actually see yourself as you see another person. This would free you from everything that now pains you.

HEAR SOMETHING HIGHER

300. Spiritual work is like hearing a different but pleasant music, where the more you listen, the more you like it.

301. There is something in us that knows when it hears the Truth.

302. You must begin to hear with something deeper than your surface mind. Until you do, you will *think* you understand, when actually you understand nothing at all.

303. To the extent that I refuse to listen to my own neurosis, I will begin to hear something above that. I will know what that something is and be it. And that something will live my life for me perfectly.

304. Your goal is to hear all the time, to never leave the wonderful feelings that come with this higher hearing.

305. When you really want to hear something outside of yourself, you will.

306. The most important thing one can hear is that "There is something wrong but it can be healed."

THE OLD-FASHIONED VIRTUES BRING HAPPINESS

307. Well, what do you know, the old-fashioned virtues are right after all. They include the wish for something higher and a willingness to learn something new.

308. Every virtue, every freedom exists because God exists.

309. Self-reliance and Truth is a marvelous combination. They blend.

310. If you want a helping hand, look at the end of your own arm.

311. Honesty is the blessed policy.

312. You can't fool an honest man.

313. I love the word clean. Truth is clean. It has nothing to do with the filth of this world. It is separate.

314. The more spiritual you become the more economical you will be. Thrift and increased understanding go hand in hand. You take only what you need, what you really need and no more.

315. Effort is a law of life.

316. Happiness belongs to the competent.

317. You're on this earth to work. Go to work!

318. Doing your work rightly in the world expands your mental powers, allowing you to rise from there to spiritual powers.

319. There are virtues and powers and I'm giving you the words that describe them. When you have the word, you can then go beyond the word itself, the sound and the writing of it, and live the word, live the meaning of it. Here are twenty very valuable words from your spiritual dictionary: attention, quietness, receptive, honesty, authentic, simplicity, release, persistence, spiritual, relaxation, healthy, choice, independence, daring, perception, logic, sincerity, reveal, awaken, pleasantness.

THE NATURAL POWER OF ENJOYMENT

320. So much depends on whether you enjoy your outer position or your inner condition.

321. Ask yourself often, "How do I feel right now?"

322. You can never enjoy your time-self. It is always a torment.

323. Would you like a true pleasure? Just be pleasant without thinking about it.

324. Have you ever thought of enjoyment as a natural power? There exists a natural and quiet enjoyment. It comes by itself as you pass beyond ego-enjoyment. Ego-enjoyment, curiously, includes feelings of guilt. You feel as if you are stealing something you have not paid for, which itself is a product of a deluded mind. Understanding this guilt can draw you away from ego-enjoyment toward the natural power of cosmic enjoyment.

REAL EXCITEMENT

325. There is destructive excitement and there is constructive excitement. You know what destructive excitement is, such as the thrill of receiving unexpected money or having power over other people.

Constructive excitement is a miraculous life-elevating experience. It consists of anything that happens to you while you are in a state of surrender to the lesson in it. The feeling that accompanies the learned lesson is constructive excitement.

326. One thing that is always right is your eagerness for something higher than yourself.

327. Every attempt to break out of yourself is a success.

328. More and more you become spiritually excited, for you are uncovering more and more secret rooms.

329. You can acquire spiritual enthusiasm. It is marvelous!

330. You'll have so much fun getting rid of yourself.

331. There is no excitement like finding the Higher Kingdom. There is no thrill like the thrill of finding your own soul.

FALSE FEELINGS OF LIFE

332. A false feeling of life is when you get the raise, when you get the woman, when you get rid of the woman, whatever, when you get an exciting feeling connected to your personal vanity.

333. Our idea of feeling good is to feel affirmed.

334. The whole tragedy of mankind is one gigantic vibration.

335. Feeling is mechanical. Knowing is conscious.

336. Evil can be defined as anything that opposes human evolvement through higher knowledge; for example, the thrill of being told you are right when you are actually wrong.

337. Thrillism is spillism.

338. Mental sickness has set up a system by which it never loses. No matter what you do and no matter what the results are, you will win an ego-victory. That means that when you send your desires out into the world: 1. You will get what you want, or 2. You won't get what you want. If you get what you want, the pseudo-nature says, "I have at last been given what I so richly deserve," and the sickness feels affirmed. If you don't get what you want, you feel sorry for yourself. You still feel affirmed because you get a feeling, and that's all that neurosis wants is a feeling.

339. Exhilaration must be followed by depression.

340. The devil is defeated as you gradually fall out of love with agitation and anger and fall in love with relaxed, right feelings.

341. A feeling makes you feel bad only because you take it as your feeling.

342. Know that you can put your life in the hands of something other than you and your false feelings.

343. God will give you a new feeling. It will be a feeling of happiness and good cheer.

LET ANXIETY GO

344. There is a state that human beings can live in that is completely free of anxiety, completely free of problems.

345. When we are inwardly ill-at-ease, we really do not see things as they are; we see them as we are.

346. The unnatural personality lives in perpetual anxiety.

347. Always seek explanation, not agitation.

348. The reason human beings are so jittery is that they are trying to pass counterfeit money.

349. Your single greatest cause of nervousness is your unawareness of it.

350. You stay nervous because you try to control it. Let go and be completely nervous with no fighting at all.

351. If you wish help in ending anxiety, the first teacher you must consult is anxiety itself. There is no way to climb the stairs toward higher teachers without first learning your first lessons from the prevailing anxiety. This means to investigate and discover the false foundation of worry and nervousness. It is like hearing a convicted robber confess that a life of crime produces only fear and tension. You understand him so clearly that you want no part of crime against others and yourself. If you have never considered anxiety as a crime against yourself, you had better start doing so—for your sake.

REPLACE CONFUSION WITH INSIGHT

352. You need not obey your swirling sea of confusion.

353. See that you're confused without doing a thing about it.

354. Your confusion is not a fixed state. Nothing has ever made it so.

355. Why on earth don't you just give up this thing that is poisoning you? Why do you love your poison? Why do you love your angry indignations? Why do you love your confusions? If you didn't love confusion, you wouldn't have it. If you were to cease to love confusion and depression, you would not have it in your life at all. Therefore, it is a reward for you.

356. Never again answer confusion when it speaks

because when you do you are caught. Be silent and the confusion will disappear.

357. Keep always in front of you this simple and good news: With right inner activity, you can replace your wounding confusion with healing insight.

THE SOLUTION TO WORRY

358. Worry occurs when a fact-thought is distorted by a self-thought.

359. My worry has nothing to do with me.

360. People worry over the absence of worry, which is like thinking that the end of the storm means the end of the sky.

361. The devil is a raging worry to himself and loves it. He therefore works fiercely to make you think that you have worries so that he can continue to masquerade as you. Your detection of this trick frees you of both the devil and his worries.

362. Loosen your grip on worry and it will loosen its grip on you.

363. No you, no future, no worry.

GETTING OUT OF YOUR OWN WAY

364. Has it ever occurred to you that you are on a collision course with yourself?

365. We are constantly fighting against our own happiness.

366. Blockage, opposition, what you call the enemy, is thought itself. You have problems. The reason you have problems is because you think you have problems. There would be no problems unless there was a person there to refer them back to an

"I," as in "I have problems." You think of ways to solve them. You think you must get back at that person who opposed you, you must win over that event. The thinking about it is the obstacle. You are using the mind to try to correct the mind. It can never be done. When you see the blockage, this insight is the action. Insight and action are the same thing.

367. Refuse to be your own obstacle any longer.

368. The hardest thing for a human being to realize is that he can't make himself happy.

369. Never give authority to a low-level impression.

370. Try to find examples where your own thought is interfering with your true interests and realize that thought has no life in itself except as you ignorantly keep it going.

371. Become an *allower* instead of a doer.

372. Reflect often on the interesting idea of getting out of your own way.

DISAPPEAR FROM YOUR LIFE

373. Don't be afraid of what is going to happen to you as a result of these studies because it can only be good, beneficial, healthy, happy, beautiful.

374. Self-abandonment and self-healing are the same thing.

375. The only thing you have to lose is the dungeon.

376. One sign of breaking the self-trap is to less and less believe in what you are talking about.

377. Notice how good you feel as you fade out of your life.

378. When I disappear to myself, I will finally live.

379. A thought comes into my mind that you have offended me, that you're not treating me right. After all, you yelled at me. This thought tells me that I have a problem. No! The only problem is my idea that I have a problem with you screaming at me. This idea came into my mind and said, "You yelled at me. I have a problem. I'd better react to it. I'd better do something about my problem."

I grabbed the idea and believed in its charlatan message. Now if I yell back, then I have a problem. If I don't yell back, I don't have a problem. And I don't have to yell back because I never had a problem to begin with. I just thought I did.

380. Anyone who does what is true and good regardless of the consequences will finally find that they are true and good for him personally.

MAKING DAILY DECISIONS

381. One of your chief torments is the making of daily decisions. You can start to end this pain by understanding just what makes a decision. What makes a decision is an idea, a belief, a thought which you wrongly take as being yourself. You therefore also wrongly think that a so-called right decision can help you and that a so-called wrong decision can harm you.

382. Right daily decisions are as simple as smiling, once you see the difference between natural and artificial needs.

383. My so-called independent decision consists merely of my dominating desire of the moment.

384. A choice made by a divided mind is surrounded and attacked by a dozen other nervous choices. But a choice made by a whole mind stands in powerful independence, for there is no alternative to a conscious choice.

385. Freedom from painful decisions is a happy result of discovering who you really are.

MONEY AND SUCCESS

386. You don't have to be a success as the world tells you that you do. God doesn't know the difference between a millionaire and a man with five cents in his pocket.

387. Because man degenerates everything he touches, the simple process of making exchanges of goods fell into the ditch like everything else he does.

388. You're supposed to be a spiritual being, not a financial one.

389. Never again use money for wrong purposes. Spend it for what you need and only for what you need.

390. The pain of lost opportunity is totally false.

391. You don't want the million dollars. You want to be free!

TRUE AND FALSE OWNERSHIP

392. You can never own anything you try to own.

393. You now do not enjoy life because you're trying to possess it. You want ownership. Your possessions are not your immortality. So make it your aim, your strong and excited aim, to enjoy life instead of possessing it. You want to collect people and houses and cars and bank accounts so that you can say, "This is mine." It's not yours, never

was, never will be, because there's no one there to own it. There's no owner of life.

394. You are not your body or your degrees.

395. It wouldn't matter if you owned the whole world. You would still have attacks of self-doubt, because you would still be suffering from the illusion that you have a self there.

396. Spiritual perception is possession.

397. You own the whole world when you no longer want to own the whole world.

398. The secret is to give up what is not your own in order to win what is not your own.

399. Be a manager, not an owner. Take your orders from God. There is nothing to own. God owns everything there is. See that there is no one there to grab and hold onto anything.

YOU ARE RESPONSIBLE

400. You have to face your responsibilities to evolve.

401. Never mind about someone else. I'm responsible for my self-work.

402. The door is always unlocked, but you must personally open it.

403. Settle for what you have and that is all you will ever have.

404. I must make the effort for myself. I am the problem. I am the solution.

405. The essence of spirituality is self-sufficiency.

406. Always return to self-responsibility. It will take you to higher and higher places.

THE FOUNTAIN OF YOUTH

407. There is a certain very insidious trap called "growing old." I want you to know that millions of human beings on earth fall into the trap of playing an old man or woman. Almost all people do it because they love playing an old person. They say, "I have contributed my part to the world, I have taken my responsibility. Now I can sit back." Never permit yourself to grow old. Your mind and spirit can always be young.

408. God is youthfulness itself.

409. The fountain of youth is in the mountain of truth.

THE SECRET OF HAPPINESS

410. If you want to be happy you must go to where happiness is.

411. Knowledge of divine nature is possible only by entering and passing through the dark tunnel of human nature. Any other way leads to self-trickery and self-isolation.

412. Let your destination unfold as God wants it to for you.

413. You will feel a new sense of health if you keep going.

414. True happiness is having the fixed knowledge that whatever comes up, you can handle it.

415. The one supreme power that will guarantee personal happiness is personal right thinking.

416. Settle for nothing less than total 100% spiritual health.

417. The entire secret for an authentically successful life can be stated very simply: Go beyond yourself.

418. Your real reward is to obey the urge to evolve.

419. Now I will tell you the secret of all secrets: There has to be a receiving without the receiver.

INNER-WORK EXERCISES

ENJOY YOUR FOOD One way to increase your intelligence is to stay awake while you eat. Be aware of your fork lifting from the table. Taste the food. Use it as an experience in spiritual growth.

ANOTHER WAY Unless you make a super effort to see that you are completely self-absorbed, you will never ever know while you are alive that there is another way to go through life where you don't say, "How is this going to affect me?" As an exercise, tomorrow, anytime, I want you to see how long you can go without mental self-involvement. When you see an object, I want you to see if you involve yourself in it. For example, "Well, I don't like watermelons."

MAKING DECISIONS Become aware of your small decisions. Lots of your decisions are based on images. You will become aware of one, two or three small decisions you have to make during the day. You will make them and say, "This is it." Then you will watch the imps coming into your mind wondering if you made the right decision. You have to refuse to listen to little imps.

THERE GOES Write "There Goes" on a piece of paper. All week long watch what is happening inside of you and say, "There goes irritation, there goes hate, there goes anger, there goes timidity," and so on.

• • •

Chapter 3
DEALING WISELY WITH OTHERS

FROM HIGH ABOVE HUMAN NATURE

420. Get along with yourself and you get along with everyone on earth.

421. There is a marvelous way to live in that you know you can handle any situation before you get there. You know you can handle any person before you meet him or any situation before it arises.

422. An eagle has nothing to say to a parrot.

423. You are not really connected with any other human being. You're not connected with any event, not really. You are whole and complete in your real nature, your actual nature. When you see that, you will know how to refuse the 10,000 problems, decisions, difficulties, pressures that come to you daily from the outside world.

424. A right relationship exists between you and another person only when your own right relationship with yourself voluntarily and naturally extends itself to the other person. All wrong relationships lack this qualification. Search it out.

425. It is possible for all your contacts and conversations with other people to flow as smoothly as a river.

THE TRUE ROAD TO RIGHT RELATIONSHIPS

426. You can't create right relationship, but you can receive it. In this thought is the secret of the ages.

427. Sweet talk makes a rough road. Strong talk makes a smooth road.

428. The trap is both inside you and outside you. You must first break the inner trap of your own delusions in order to be free of the outer trap. An example of breaking only the outer trap is to get rid of a harmful person without also gaining insight from the experience. In this case, you will sooner or later fall into the trap of another harmful human relationship.

429. Self-deception allows others to deceive us.

430. The inner always reflects itself in the outer.

431. Because you attribute nonexistent virtues to yourself, you also attribute them to others.

432. If you really understand human nature, you will know everything needed to know to live skillfully in this world. But if you merely pretend to know human nature, you will be the helpless victim of people and events. Now do you think it worthwhile to really understand human nature?

433. You're relying on people who don't have self-reliance.

434. Everyone is either on the upward path or the downward path.

435. If you were really on the upward path, you would be too happy all day to be bad and mean.

436. When living correctly with yourself, you will know exactly how to live in right relationship with others.

THE ONLY THING YOU OWE ANYONE

437. The only thing you owe anyone is a mature nature.

438. If you do not have a good and mature relationship with yourself, it is foolish to think you can have a good and mature relationship with another person.

439. You see, it is not selfish to live your life as you see fit; it is selfish only to insist that others live as you see fit.

440. You are not required to act in any way that sacrifices your wish to grow in spiritual strength. For example, you are not required to support the weakness of another person. Also, you are not required to relieve the anxiety of anyone whose anxiety is caused by his preference for delusion over reality.

441. You will feel much better by realizing that the other person must live according to his own real or imaginary interests, not according to your demands.

442. Instead of letting other people's troubles fall on your shoulders, let them fall on your understanding.

443. When someone invites you to join him in the mental slums, refuse the invitation. You must remain alert to do this. Build a list of your own examples of your refusal to go slumming. For instance, you may feel that someone has a silent grudge toward you. Refuse to be made uncomfortable over his descent into psychological slums.

444. There is such a thing as a normal and natural dislike of another person in which the dislike has no wrongness or hostility in it. It is a state in which a certain rightness in you wants nothing to do with a certain wrongness in another person. Rightness is calmly repelled by wrongness, as when you decline to approach someone with a cold and suspicious manner.

445. People are sheeple, but a real person stands out like a man among statues.

THE SLAVERY OF APPROVAL

446. You have problems with people for the prime reason that you want something from them.

447. You want their approval because you aren't pleased with yourself.

448. We are often attracted by those who damage us. Of course, we have already damaged ourselves. This self-damage reaches out and allies itself with its own kind. I am attracted to what is like me.

449. Your behavior makes me feel what I am. If you marry me, I feel wanted. If you don't, I feel rejected.

450. Approval from other people is trash.

451. Appeasement is disaster.

452. If you want anyone to tell you that you are right you are wrong.

453. The only way to truly not care what others think of you is to truly know that you are right.

454. See the pain in trying to live up to what others expect of you. Then see that there is always a concealed threat in back of their expectations. Then see that the threat exists because of the wrong operation of both your mind and your behavior. Then see you can set yourself free by loosening one knot each day.

455. Endure the discomfort of not doing what another expects of you. When you see why something happened to you psychologically and pay attention to it, it will not happen again.

456. When you know you're not you, the last thing you're going to do is to look to someone else to give you a little smile, to tell you how great you are, because you're tired of playing the game.

457. Stop caring what other people think of you. Only care what God thinks of you.

DON'T BE DECEIVED

458. He didn't know the answer, so he talked endlessly about the answer.

459. The bigger the faker, the bigger the acher.

460. He is too sick to know that he is sick.

461. They are stuck in the mud and they want to stay there.

462. He is the kind of man who wants his modesty known by everyone on earth.

463. The only difference between sleeping people is the way they snore.

464. Men who fall from a canoe while standing up to attract attention always claim someone pushed them.

465. If you don't want to suffer like most people you can't be like most people.

ORDERS FROM ABOVE

466. The only thing you must do to be reborn is to collapse.

467. Never use the word love again until you know from yourself what it means.

468. Stay away from people who love being victims.

469. Let the spiritual direct the social.

470. You are absolutely forbidden to help any human being who is crying hysterically and shaking themselves apart.

471. Starting now, never again permit hard or disapproving facial expressions to intimidate you.

472. No more weak smiles!

473. You are forbidden to put pressure on another human being in order to get what you want from him or her.

ABOUT RUDENESS

474. The invented self is rudeness itself.

475. There is a definite connection between mental sickness and bad manners. Watch for the connection. As you mingle with people, watch how neurosis frequently lashes out at people with contemptuous behavior and outrageous demands. The problem is that mental sickness never sees bad manners as bad manners, which is what keeps it sick and bad.

476. Unpleasant behavior is sick behavior. Few people want to think about this fact, but you will do so. From now on, you will see that unpleasant people are sick people. You know the thousand varieties of unpleasantness including sarcastic accusations, delirious demands, repulsive self-worship, a cold and hostile face. If another person is unpleasant, realize that your wish for sunlight must have nothing to do with his darkness.

477. An inconsiderate person does not see how much unnecessary work he selfishly piles on others. Not seeing this fact, he hurts with disbelieving indignation when told about it.

478. People are surly and rude because their attention is locked in the downward position. They have become what they have attended to.

479. Plain and simple courteous behavior? Self-centeredness never heard of it.

480. Courtesy can't be explained to a rude mind.

481. Connect suffering with rudeness.

482. If your behavior is unpleasant, you must see that you have chosen midnight over noon and see that you will stumble and fall in your own darkness.

483. The only way to have good manners is to wake up.

TO BE NICE AND PLEASANT

484. The only way to be nice is to be real.

485. You think you are grouchy only when you act grouchily, when in fact your basic nature is that of a grouch. Your exterior pleasantness is that of an anticipating hawk who watches and waits for something to pounce on.

486. Have the courtesy and decency to let other people think the thoughts they want to think instead of you imposing your thoughts on them. The reason you do this—yelling, interrupting and wanting to be the center of the conversation—is because you want to try to prove to yourself that your thoughts are real, that they are important and that they back up a very real person.

487. Real niceness does not have a motive.

488. When that false, infantile nature which used to like to win has been removed from your life, you have

a niceness that you never knew before. You have a patience, you have a kindness, you have an insight that you don't have to work to keep in place. You know that this is the truly permanent power and strength and intelligence. This is the right position, where you have no position at all. Now the unnamed you has a position which God Himself has given you, but you have no concern with keeping it in place or keeping it strong.

489. If you can't help but be a generally gloomy human being, here is something you might find hard to believe. The day can come when you can't help but be a nice and pleasant and cheerful human being.

490. Get rid of all those foreign invaders who inhabit your inner castle and you will be as nice all the time as you are some of the time.

491. Real niceness is spiritual insight.

CONSCIENCE AND COMPASSION

492. You care for others in the right way when you no longer care for yourself in the wrong way.

493. If you do not give others strength, you give them weakness.

494. It is impossible for weakness to have conscience or consideration towards others.

495. Parents pass on to their children their actual natures.

496. The father who does not correct his child does not care for that child. He wants him to grow up just like he is.

497. Compassion is the non-toleration of darkness in another person.

498. Maybe you can forgive someone who has injured you. But see if you can forgive someone whom you have injured.

499. You are not required to listen to anyone who demands, "What are you doing about my problems?"

500. One sign of a sick mind is its evil delight in causing trouble to others and it leaps eagerly upon the slightest opportunity to do so. A healthy mind, having a real conscience, alertly avoids causing trouble to others, though the others are rarely aware of it.

501. People who have finally decided to waste their lives in concealed hostility are totally dedicated to wasting your life also. They have no conscience whatever in spreading the wastage and wreckage from them to you and they do it with devilish cunning. Vow now that you will understand this so deeply that no one will ever again be able to waste your life.

502. Always remember the following fact: Anyone who is a burden to you receives secret and sinister pleasure from burdening you. Your only duty toward him is to quietly and absolutely refuse to be burdened by him. Understand that this gives him the only chance he has for lifting the burden he is to himself.

503. Please people and you achieve nothing, but please your real self and you start a miracle.

504. Make it your number one wish in life to expose human evil and free yourself from it. Human evil is very carefully concealed. Evil, weakness, is what makes your life so difficult. If you have this one wish, you will have a very real experience of changing yourself from a taker to a giver. Now you're nothing but a taker. Taking is the curse. Takers have no conscience.

THE LAW OF LEVELS

505. We demand that other people behave better only because we don't understand a certain spiritual law: One cannot act above his actual level. So don't expect others to behave better. They won't and they can't.

506. Don't expect immature minds to be interested in mature topics.

507. What you really are connects with the people and events with the same actual condition.

508. It is a psychological law: If you get your feelings hurt frequently and intensely, you like to frequently and intensely hurt the feelings of others. Your lack of realization of this does not make it any less true.

509. Whatever you get from a man or woman is the answer to the prayer of your present level of being.

510. The Law of Levels is absolute.

511. We must leave the lower to have the higher.

512. When you become spiritual you raise the level of the entire world.

SILENT ANSWERS TO OTHERS FROM TRUTH

513. On Monday you were cruel and on Tuesday you said you were sorry. But on Wednesday you did it again, which means I'm not going to believe anything you say on Thursday.

514. Who says I owe you something except your own personal self-interest? The next time someone declares or hints that you owe him something, give him an accurate reply. Say to him, "If you are looking for someone to unload your complaints on, look for someone else. I will not participate in your self-injury."

515. There must be something wrong with my ear—it can't keep up with your mouth.

516. Whatever gave you the notion that I will tolerate an unpleasant relationship?

517. If you want to go crazy, go all by yourself. You are wasting your time trying to haul me into your craziness.

518. When I tell you that I don't want to do something that you want me to do, that settles the matter once and for all. I am not required to explain to you why I don't want to do it and I won't.

519. Sorry, but I don't permit your nonsense to judge me.

520. If you are incapable of pleasant behavior, stay out of my life.

521. You had better behave decently in my company or you're not going to be in my company.

522. Sorry, but you are wasting your time trying to make me feel responsible for your desperation. You will of course call me cold-hearted, but I know that your desperation is black-hearted.

523. If you know what is best for me, why are you so miserable?

524. I took the time to see that my problem with you was really my problem with myself. It secured a very interesting result. I now also see clearly that your problem with me is really your problem with yourself.

525. One day you may meet an old friend and silently say to him, "You don't know it, but you are not talking with the same man you used to know."

526. Gentleness and kindness is the essence of the true relationship between men and women.

527. The real and only reward of being a man or a woman is to be fully a man or a woman.

528. God has given to every human being the same opportunity to climb to the spiritual heights.

529. God has no favorites. His full power is given to each human being who wants it. Nothing is held back. He gives you all the blessings and grace of the entire kingdom.

530. How it goes: A woman will be mean to a weak man; a weak man will be mean to a woman. A woman cannot be mean to a strong man; a strong man cannot be mean to a woman.

531. The man must be in charge in male-female relationships.

532. Where the wife is the boss, there is spiritual loss.

533. Your dinner companion who gives trouble to the waitress is just dying to give trouble to you.

534. A man doesn't care how unfashionable he is as long as he's comfortable. A woman doesn't care how uncomfortable she is as long as she's fashionable.

535. We switch from one wrong relationship to another because we are wrong. We call it marriage or romance and it is mutual destruction.

536. Always enter relationships on your own terms of rightness, never on anyone else's.

537. The vast majority of your relationships with the opposite sex should begin at twelve noon and end one second after twelve.

538. It is often a painful process for a man and a woman to come to a parting of the ways. I will show you how to pull all the pain out of it. When the other person says goodbye, simply and casually wave goodbye in return. If he never returns to say hello again, that ends the matter and you need never give it another thought. But if he returns to say hello again, you can then decide whether or not you wish to return the hello. This simple formula keeps you in charge of all possibilities.

539. No one loves me? What has that to do with me?

540. When the love for Truth precedes the love for William or Mary, then the love for William or Mary is genuine. But of course, from the higher viewpoint, there is no difference between the two loves. There is only one love.

541. The real part of a man falls in love with the real part of a woman.

542. When Truth knows what to do with me, I will know what to do with the opposite sex.

FOR MEN

543. Men, if you want to be free, you'll have to be free of every woman you meet.

544. Find yourself before you find a woman, after which you will know what to do with what you have found.

545. Tell a woman fifty times that you like her, after which she will pause three seconds and then ask, "Yes, but do you still like me?"

546. Men have the primary responsibility in making a relationship work. Men are the active force.

547. A man takes the lead and makes decisions.

548. Any man who submits to a bossy woman is no man.

549. A man who loves Truth more than he loves a woman truly loves that woman and that woman will love him.

550. My dear lady, would it surprise you to learn that I place Truth ahead of your sexual favors?

551. God is what a real and true man acts from. A real man could never place a woman under the least bit of anxiety.

552. Only a spiritual man is a real man.

FOR WOMEN

553. Any woman who wants a man is properly feminine.

554. It is natural for a woman to be intelligently and consciously passive toward a man, which is not submission. There is no such thing as domination and submission in a right man-woman relationship.

555. A woman should be passive toward her husband and active toward her child.

556. A woman loves a man whose relationship with her may or may not include sex, but definitely includes a power of his to protect her.

557. One part of a woman wants to dominate the man, while another part of her prays she will fail.

558. It is right and natural, not weak and irresponsible, for a woman to want a man to take care of her.

559. God never condemned a woman to be trapped with a wrong man.

560. It is normal and natural and therefore nice, for a woman to want to be held by a strong man, held both physically and spiritually.

ABOUT SEX

561. When you have no dreams of any kind about love and romance, your love life will be perfect.

562. Be aware of confused and painful attitudes toward sex and the opposite sex, but do not fear them.

563. Anyone tyrannized by wrong sex ideas will always take his wrong ideas as his correct understanding of sex.

564. Sex can be a real pleasure, very relaxed, completely relaxed, when you can take it or leave it.

565. The only kind of sex compatible with self-awakening is natural, normal sex between a man and a woman.

566. When a truly mature man has sex with a woman, it is the same with him as if he had lunch with her. Afterward he casually remarks to the woman, "That was very nice," while referring to either the sex or the salad.

567. Sex is connected with all other parts of these studies.

568. If you are not dependent upon another to give you what you lack, then your natural sex impulses fall into place with no effort on your part.

TRUST

569. Don't trust anything of human origin. You trust because you don't know. When you know, there is no need to trust. Knowing is life, trusting is death.

570. Use your next crisis to reveal what you have been trusting in.

571. You never really trust another person. You trust your judgment about them.

572. When you quietly admit that you do not know a particular answer about life, notice that you now know your emptiness. This kind of knowing changes everything.

573. Finally you'll get smart enough to see what it means to trust God. Your new aim will be to get up in the morning wide awake, trying to see the devils that are trying to drag you down. There is great purity in the force of Truth.

ABOUT ENEMIES

574. Invisible evil is the enemy, not that person or event.

575. The enemy is always within, never out there.

576. An awakened man has no enemies even if he has enemies.

577. You never really hate another person. Believing that you hate him is another type of cunning self-deception. What you really hate is the weakness in yourself that is revealed by the other person's rejection of you. This principle contains the secret of liberty from all wrong human relations.

578. When you hear your enemy criticized and you feel pleasure over it, there is something seriously wrong with you. It is possible to know that you or another person is faulty without falling into any kind of self-centered reaction.

579. There's no one to attack. There's no one to defend. You don't know that yet. If you knew that, you'd be off the battlefield.

580. After long hard work on yourself you will look inside and all your enemies will have disappeared. Now for the final shock. You look inside and *you* have disappeared! It had to happen. It's a two-way singular process.

581. God has no enemies. You do!

582. Let God take care of your enemies. He knows how, you don't.

DETECT WRONG BEHAVIOR

583. Ignorance of human nature is a delight to evil human nature. Evil human nature operates and injures people only when people are ignorant of its nature.

584. Try to detect how other people tell you the kind of people they are. For example, when talking to others, they tell you how they don't have a minute to spare. They are saying, "I am an important and busy person."

585. When someone tells you what they are, they're telling you what they are not.

586. Nothing is easier than self-destruction. All you have to do is get mad when told the truth about yourself.

587. We are cosmic cops.

588. Detect forced behavior.

589. We are enslaved by a desire to make a good impression.

590. You're spending all your time trying to find someone to be nicer to you than you are to yourself.

591. No one is meaner to you than you are to yourself.

592. If you suffer, you are wrong.

593. Admitting you're wrong is detecting the devil.

594. Do one thing, have one aim: Detect human evil and be free of it.

DON'T LET PEOPLE DRAG YOU INTO THEIR PROBLEMS

595. Let's go into business together. With my brains and your money, we can really go places.

596. You are an extremely rude and selfish person. I wish to intrude into your life and your affairs to get what I want and you have the discourtesy to refuse me.

597. I want to be reasonable about this so I've come up with the following fair deal. My part will be to criticize whatever you do. Your part will be to come up with plans more pleasing to me.

598. It is your moral duty to make my decisions for me, but of course it is my moral duty to hate you for any decisions I don't like.

599. If it turns out good, I did it. If it turns out bad, you did it.

600. I don't understand what you are saying so the only intelligent thing to do is to attack you.

601. I have your sarcasm. Now please give me your intelligent helpfulness.

602. If you have the same sickness I have, you are marvelous. If you have a different sickness, you are weird.

603. When someone speaks to you about something,

you don't have to be dragged into it. Just leave it alone. Practice being in this life and not permitting your weakness to let another drag you off. You can develop yourself to the point where you can hear every bit of bad news that has ever existed since the founding of civilization on earth, all the bad news that is presently on earth and all the prophesied bad news, and be unaffected by it.

604. First, he *politely requests* that you solve his problems for him. If you agree, he next *demands* that you solve his problems for him. If you agree, he then *threatens you with injury* if you fail to solve his problems for him. If you agree, he finally *hates and attacks* you for not solving his problems for him. Where you made your first big mistake was to fail to simply walk away after his first request.

605. Sorry, but you will never convince me that the problem you invited is my problem to chase away. Never. I now see too much to fall for that. I see that the only one who can end his problem is the same one who started it. This is a spiritual and psychological law.

RELIEF FROM GRIEF WITH OTHERS

606. Handling a person or an event correctly really means to not handle them at all but to let your mature nature understand everything that goes on without personal involvement.

607. The most dangerous words on earth are, "Let me help you."

608. Don't fall into other people's remarks.

609. Do-gooders are do-badders.

610. Permitting your life to be taken over by another person is like letting the waiter eat your dinner.

611. What I'm about to tell you will save you many, many hours of grief: Keep your own personal life private and don't let anyone in except on the terms you have allowed Reality to set up in you.

612. Never tell vultures what you plan to have for lunch. If you tell them you are having coleslaw, they will swoop down and corner the cabbage market.

613. Sneering is a characteristic of a vicious animal, not of a decent human being. Now you can easily detect an animal masquerading as a human being.

614. See how neurotic people try to drain your energy by trying to get you involved with what is bothering them.

615. Forget about what other people do with their life. You are here on earth for inner growth, to connect yourself with God.

616. It is a bright day when we see that cosmic facts are as practical as a recipe for baking bread.

FREEDOM FROM WHAT OTHERS THINK

617. Think of how you would feel if you really didn't care what other people think of you. Think of the tremendous burden that would be dropped from your back.

618. When you are dependent on the higher, you are independent of the lower.

619. Your problem is you are thinking about what other people are thinking about you. Your thinking about what they're thinking is your thought. It belongs to

you. You think about other people and about how they think toward you in order to make your existence seem real.

620. When thinking toward anyone you have hurt in the past, you say everything necessary by saying silently to him, "You will never really know how sorry I am. You will never really know because you don't know how asleep I was. But I know and I am so sorry about it that I am free from all guilt and pain. I guarantee you it will never happen again. Rather, Truth guarantees it will never happen again."

621. Shed the influence of the last person you met.

622. When are you free of someone? When you don't think about them at all.

BEWARE!

623. Anyone who sees himself as a hammer will see you as a nail.

624. An insane human being wants you to doubt your present false position so that he can replace it with his own self-serving false position. A sane human being wants you to doubt your present false position so that you can replace it with the effortless ways of sanity.

625. From time to time you will hear someone starting an accusation with the phrase, "But you told me...." When hearing this, know that you are hearing someone who demands that you think for him but who is eager to blame you when things go wrong.

626. Tell a vicious person that he is vicious and watch how quickly he proves the point.

627. It is ten times easier to protect yourself from your enemies than from your friends.

628. Beware of a man whose stupidity is his pride, whose revenge is his entertainment, whose weakness is his power. A man whose heaven is his hell has nothing but the viciousness of hell to give you.

629. Any human being who tries to make you feel guilty is an evil human being and don't you listen to him.

WATCH OUT FOR WOLVES

630. On Monday an enthusiastic sheep taught a class of wolves on the topic of vegetarianism and its benefits. On Tuesday the class was discontinued for lack of a teacher.

631. A foolish rabbit entered the den of the king of wolves to complain about his vicious treatment from other wolves.

632. Going into the meadow, a wolf solemnly promised the sheep that he would stop attacking them. With great relief the sheep accepted the wolf's repentance. Sure enough the attacks vanished, for so had the sheep.

633. Only an insane mind tries to bring peace between two other insane minds.

634. By eliminating the sheep in himself, a man gives psychic wolves nothing to prey upon.

635. God wants to give you a nature that will scare the wolves away. When they see you coming they start running.

THE ONLY WAY TO HELP OTHERS

636. There is true caring for others when you are consciously intolerant of the behavior by which they are wrecking themselves.

637. You place yourself in great personal danger when you are mechanically kindly and helpful to a lost person. And if you don't try to understand what this means, you will find yourself in danger when it is too late to save yourself from injury at the hands of the lost person. Lost people are totally treacherous.

638. When an unconscious person tries to help another unconscious person, the unconscious helper gets bitten and it hurts. When a conscious person tries to help an unconscious person, the conscious helper also gets bitten but it does not hurt.

639. The overwhelming insistence of your own desires prevents you from seeing and understanding the desires of the other person. This causes conflict for your unseen state arrogantly insists that the other person must think and act in the only way that exists to you—your own self-centered way.

640. The only way you can help another is to help him raise his level.

TRUTH ABOVE ALL

641. Place no one, nothing, above the Spirit of Truth.

642. Stop being afraid of this sick world. Stop it! That man or woman can't do a thing to you, not if you really understand. You have nothing, nothing to protect.

643. Learn to take the side of rightness instead of the side of a person.

644. The way to inner success is utterly simple. Just do what is unpopular but right.

645. Let this statement penetrate you until you begin to live it: If I have to be the only person on earth to stand on the side of Trueness, then I'll do it because I want it more than anything else.

646. Always remember that God keeps His promises.

647. You'll have it made in a way that you never thought was possible. You'll know who to associate with and who you should not associate with.

648. It is as possible to be pleasantly alone with yourself while surrounded by a crowd as it is to walk alone in the peaceful woods.

649. There is a lofty feeling, inexpressible in words, a state in which you in your spiritual wisdom know that you are really not alone at all.

650. Some day you will be so grateful for these truths that all you can say all day is, "Thank you, thank you!"

651. The Truth first, last and always.

INNER-WORK EXERCISES

SHAKE YOURSELF AWAKE All you do is doze. You have to shake yourself awake. If all you have is a physical body, start with that. For the next three days, wherever you are, continually shake your head awake. Supply the necessary number of jolts to show yourself you've been sound asleep.

IS IT ME OR...? Every time you converse with another, turn your attention to your own words. Listen to yourself talk and ask yourself, "Is the center of my conversation me or the other person?"

SPIRITUAL DETECTIVE As an alert spiritual detective, detect your words and thoughts and actions and listen to yourself talk to any person, anywhere, anytime, with a wish to be instructed by the Spirit of Truth. Watch the revelation come that that was insecurity talking. Watch both verbal and mental statements and, seeing your actual state, know there is an alternative. We're here to banish self-torment. Want to do it? Do the exercise!

GET YOUR LIFE BACK How deeply we are in love with trying not to disappoint people so as to retain our self-image of being nice and kindly. We will sacrifice anything to get approval. We don't need to be afraid of displeasing people. There are little phrases we use such as, "Oh, I don't mind." You *do* mind. Effective as of now, you will find small ways to dare to disappoint people who want something from you. Go home and make a list of small things that you are afraid to do and do them when the opportunity arises. Get ten or fifteen. For example: 1. Please return this to me, Mary. 2. No, I can't take your children to school. It doesn't matter what happens, start doing something right for yourself.

• • •

Chapter 4
YOUR SPIRITUAL ADVENTURE

A CLASS IN COSMIC CLIMBING

652. The spiritual adventure is the only fun there is.

653. Anything that does not lead you higher is lifeless.

654. If there is one sentence I could say to the whole world it would be, "Why settle for chaos when you don't have to?"

655. If we had to select one word that is essential, prominent and necessary regarding our life here on earth, that one word would be growth.

656. The growth of your physical body was handed to you. But spiritual growth is not handed to you. You must work for it.

657. We grow only through exposure of foolishness.

658. Spiritual knowledge, followed by self-surrender, develops what is real within.

659. The purpose of life is not to follow the pain deeper and deeper into yourself but to climb out!

660. You can live in a high spiritual state where you know that all is well, for all is well with God and God is now living His life through you.

661. Climb!

DISCOVER WHAT MUST BE DONE

662. You don't have to create your own life.

663. All you have to do is agree with Truth.

664. Do not try to discover who you are. Find out who you are not.

665. Believing in your invented identity is the same as believing in your defeat.

666. The mind becomes corrupt whenever it calls itself anything.

667. Be correction-minded.

668. If you lose something wrong, you will find something right.

669. Recognize the emptiness of every direction you take, and that will give you the wish to be overwhelmed by something that is not of this world.

670. There are three steps to finding Truth: You listen, you hear, you obey.

671. Here is how it goes on the path to Truth: hearing, fearing, peering, nearing, clearing, cheering.

A SOURCE OF REFRESHING ENERGY

672. The energy that causes you to raise your arm created the universe. This should startle and shock you in the right way.

673. Higher energy can do something that nothing else can do. What it can do is conquer the universe.

674. Just now we have neurotic energy, hatred, etc. God's energy is pure but it is distorted on the intellectual level.

675. We are expressers of the energy that comes from either the good or the bad place.

676. A conscious refusal to divert your energies into lower-level activities is a special command that turns your energies into higher-level spiritual success.

677. Do not follow the deceitful lures of distress and disappointment.

678. Right initiative comes from seeing your condition as it actually is. The seeing of that arouses great energy.

THE PAIN OF EGOTISM

679. The problem is not a what, the problem is a who. And guess who?

680. Interesting how both ignorance and insolence start with the letter "I."

681. There is no limit to the pain that egotism will cause when feeling cornered and threatened—and it always has this feeling.

682. I annoy me.

683. Maybe the world is suffering from that weird little sickness known as (fill in your name)-itis.

684. You think you're talking about something real when you talk about yourself. You're not. You're a fiction calling yourself real, calling yourself solid. Who are you? Tell me who you are. You haven't the slightest notion. If you don't have a central self, which you don't, then you don't have to take care of it because there's nothing to take care of, right? You're trying to take care of something that exists only in your delusion, in your imagination.

685. Do you really think it is possible to improve an illusion?

686. There is Goodness, but you want to be God and wreck it all.

687. When the wretched self searches, it finds the wretched self.

688. Authentic goodness is the absence of the habitual me.

689. Feel sorry for yourself rightly by feeling sorry that you have a self.

690. Your egotism is costing you eternal life.

691. May I remind you that you are not the only person in the world to have problems?

692. Prayer: Dear God please help me. Please help me to fade out of my own life.

THE REAL PATH TO FREEDOM

693. Freedom is freedom from unconscious thinking.

694. The unfamiliar is the gateway to freedom.

695. You're not good. You're not bad. You're nothing. That nothing is everything. Now you have enough to think about for a week.

696. When you tell yourself you're no one you're telling yourself the most freeing fact in the world.

697. Inner-liberation can be described as a condition in which you no longer take either credit or blame for anything.

698. You can be who you think you are or who God says you are.

699. There is a *me* self and there is a *free* self.

700. The only thing I need is freedom from myself.

TELL TRUTH YOU'RE SORRY

701. It is always beneficial to tell the Truth that you are sorry for your self-defeating behavior. When motivated by the simple recognition and admission

that you have been wrong, it is a wise and healthy act. However, your first timid resolve to say you are sorry will arouse furious opposition. This opposition is the devil himself. The devil is never more cunningly evil than when warning you against an honest apology, threatening you with mysterious and ghastly consequences.

You must not listen to his lies, which are manufactured in the hell of time-thinking. Here is what this means. In the past you have apologized to people who twisted your apology to serve their own sick needs; for example, their reaction was a sneering pounce. The devil warns you against getting hurt again in this way.

But remember, never forget, that you are now talking with Truth not to devil-dominated human beings. Truth is different. It can never be anything but understanding, compassionate and truly helpful. It always welcomes a contrite heart. So be both humble and bold in telling the Truth that you are sorry. Truth will nod briefly in approval, then hand you the next section of the map that leads to the top of the mountain.

UNDEVELOPED ABILITIES

702. You don't understand that you have undeveloped abilities.

703. We have the power of attention, of interest, even the power of physical movement. All these powers must be brought together in a concentrated force.

704. You must catch your old nature before it leaps into a challenge, event or crisis.

705. Attend to what matters, not to what scatters.

706. When the heart is right, the mind and the emotions will follow.

707. One day all your right parts will come together.

START WITH THE PHYSICAL BODY

708. The perfect place to start is with physical things. One center tends to follow another.

709. Place your physical body on your own side in your upward climb. Let it serve your true needs like being at every class, reading, walking with awareness, everything!

710. Relax. Dare to not be so tense. It is not necessary.

711. Relaxation brings recognition.

712. Write this down and never forget it: The body is not you.

713. To be a spiritual human being is the single most important thing you can do for your ordinary health.

714. It is possible for your physical body to be inspired by Heaven, so that you go to right places, you do right things.

STRENGTH AND WEAKNESS

715. Learn to understand that there are values that last far beyond time into eternity. Everything in time is weakness, is evil, is harmful to you. So be disloyal to your sick nature and say *NO* to your sick thoughts and to human sickos who seek to wreck you. The Spirit of Truth, which is strength, is available. It is possible to listen and learn and become strong.

716. A truly strong person does not need the approval of others anymore than a lion needs the approval of sheep.

717. By being weak you are contributing to the awful condition of this world.

718. The reason you are internally mixed up, chaotic, hurting all the time, is because you are weak when you could be strong.

719. Growing up into the fullness of inner strength is as exciting as seeking gold and as rewarding as finding it.

720. You don't have to think about how to be strong anymore. The only strength that exists is the strength of not being you anymore.

721. The self-rejecters call themselves modest, but they are dangerously conceited. The self-accepters call themselves confident, but they are foolishly weak. Only the absence of self-thought is modest and confident.

722. If you were utterly, utterly weak you would have the strength of the universe.

723. I will direct my strength towards self-understanding.

724. Noticing every thought and action is the same thing as asking God to be your strength.

THE UNIQUE REWARDS OF INNER WORK

725. Beginners along the spiritual path make a fundamental mistake. They think that the higher rewards are nothing more than a variation of earthly rewards.

726. You are always receiving glimpses of Truth, but you are unconscious of them.

727. You can have so much good, so much of God in your life, that crises and inner problems are stopped before they have a chance to form.

728. Oh, how easy your life will be when you are sane.

729. When I am no longer hard-hearted, hard work is easy.

730. There are three stages that a spiritual traveler passes through: 1. The collection of information and ideas, 2. The personal experiencing of what you collect, and 3. The direct inspiration and instruction from the originator of all inspiration and instruction.

731. You can feel so good that you never want to leave your own company.

732. You must perform your spiritual exercises without prophesying the nature of your reward. If you have a preconceived notion of the reward, you may or may not get it but the very desire for that reward blocks the higher reward which is above all mental prophecy. As you actually receive a few higher rewards and your cosmic confidence rises, you feel from yourself that this way, which was at first so strange and frightening, is the way of endless riches.

733. There will come a point where you acknowledge your gratefulness for the patience of God in putting up with you.

DEFEAT WHAT NOW DEFEATS YOU

734. What I am about to say is supported by psychology, religion and just plain common sense: the inner determines the outer.

735. If fierce dragons constantly appear and disappear in your life, your own mind is the mad magician.

736. Aim to understand the dragon, not defeat him, for to understand the dragon is his defeat.

737. Defeat has no right to exist.

SEE WHERE YOU ARE WRONG

738. Since logic is a sure road to rightness, a wrongness-loving person will refuse to travel it. A spiritually wrong person is incapable of even elementary logic, for he senses that logic will take him away from himself. And since he loves only himself, he must dodge and despise logic.

739. If you can talk a monkey out of a banana, you can talk logic with someone whose self-interest rejects logic.

740. Vanity can't stand spiritual logic.

741. If I am agitated, I am wrong.

742. You can speed up life correction with the following method: The next time it happens, remember what happened the last time it happened.

743. If you continue to operate from the same cause, you will have the same effects.

744. The following fact occurs to only one mind in a million: When someone is punished for bad behavior, it is also for bad behavior against himself.

745. Your wrongness is your present idea of happiness. Try to see how it is wrecking your life. You have one real chance. That one chance is to find yourself wrong. Never forget the first sentence of this paragraph, which is, your wrongness is your present idea of happiness. Replace that idea.

746. Always stay on the path of seeing what is wrong. Then you will see what is right.

STOP SUPPLYING YOUR ANSWERS

747. You cannot and must not answer your own questions. You fail to see that you are doing this when you look outside yourself for wisdom or strength or guidance. You are like the king of a castle who falls off his horse while riding in the woods. In his dazed state he wanders into a cave thinking it is his home, even while suffering from the cave's discomfort. As his head gradually clears, he remembers where he truly belongs. Then his action in understanding guides him back to the castle with its true security and comfort.

748. Don't ask the terrifying question and you won't need a comforting answer.

749. A self-tormenting question is a wrong question. Drop it right now.

750. The reason there is so much wrong with the question is because there is so much wrong with the questioner.

751. When you don't know something and stick with that unknowing, there is no conflict. Conflict occurs when you don't understand something about life but pretend that you do by grabbing your own answers.

752. All wrong answers are in time.

753. A wise man explained how he became wise: "I never answered my own questions."

754. A quiet mind knows the answer, which means we must cease to fight anxiously for the answer.

755. Here is a prayer that will always attract an answer: "I don't even know what I need to know, so please start helping me at this point."

756. Whatever the question, I will not supply my own pet answer. I will remember that I am a student in the cosmic classroom, not the teacher.

RISE ABOVE THINKING IN OPPOSITES

757. We dwell in the part of the mind that thinks in opposites.

758. Ordinary human life is described by two alternating sentences: This is it! This is not it. Need I say more?

759. The intellect can only move back and forth, never upward.

760. True life is vertical, not horizontal.

761. Your attitudes divide themselves into two camps: self-love and self-hate.

762. You condemn yourself because you first approve yourself.

763. Think of the most evil, degenerate person you know. I guarantee you that that person sees himself the exact opposite of what he is.

764. You are saved when you invite spiritual perception, which will give you spiritual renewal and spiritual discovery, the discovery being that Truth, God, resides above the way your mind operates in opposites. You rise above the opposites and Truth is there. You rise above them and your new nature is there. Your true nature is above your mind. Event-

ually you won't think about spirituality. You will know it, you will have it and you will live it.

GO AGAINST THE MECHANICAL FLOW

765. Your purpose is to understand the cranking of the machine inside you that goes on without your knowledge.

766. Ignorance is a mechanical force.

767. Never trust a dangerous machine for you could get hurt. This includes a machine having wheels and gears and bolts or a machine having eyes and ears and arms.

768. Don't mechanically follow the moods of other people.

769. You take the lead and create the mood with everyone you meet.

770. The *it* in you is doing all those things that are done in your life. The *it* performs all your actions, no doubt about that. The only way to tell the difference between the good things and the bad things that are done is to take the *you* out of the *it*. Then, once understanding the mental *it,* you will do everything only from the Cosmic It, which is the naturally flowing action of Reality.

771. Let's see what that machine says and does today.

BLABBERMOUTHERY

772. Beware the yap trap—inwardly and outwardly.

773. You will see spiritual truths much more clearly by using your eyes instead of your mouth.

774. Stop blabbing and just notice what you are doing right now. Divided attention is no attention. Stop blabbing and just notice what you are doing right now.

775. Deliberately rob yourself of the pleasure of making that remark. Go through the hell of not saying what your old nature wants you to say. For instance, somebody is talking about where they've been and you want to say, "I've been there too," and so on.

776. You really understand it when you are not compelled to talk about it.

777. Your silence cannot give out its wisdom as long as your mouth is giving out its nonsense.

778. The next time you want to tell somebody about your car, your house, your plumbing, etc., stop and don't do it. Be conscious of how others talk incessantly to you about their interests.

779. When I ask you a question, will you please tell me what I need to know, not what you want to talk about?

780. I phoned you to ask a practical question about a necessary matter. This took five seconds. You then told me about your cousin in Kansas who keeps a pet pig. This took ten minutes. I phoned you to ask a practical question about a necessary matter. This took seven seconds. You then told me about your childhood victory of being able to climb higher into the sycamore tree than anyone else. This took twelve minutes. I phoned you to ask a practical question about a necessary matter. This took ten seconds. You then gave me detailed information on telling the difference between a butterfly and a moth. This took fourteen minutes. I just turned on my kitchen

faucet to watch the water gush forth with full force—which reminds me to not ask you any more questions.

BE A THOUGHT-WATCHER

781. Know what you're thinking, second by second.

782. There are four categories of thought: 1. Wicked thoughts. 2. Wasteful thoughts. 3. Practical thoughts. 4. Spiritual thoughts.

783. A bad thought will always cause a bad feeling and a bad physical action.

784. Worried thought prevents practical thought which could prevent worried thought.

785. We will make swift progress up to heaven when we understand that a thought can't change a thought, when we see that ego-centered thinking can bring no solutions.

786. Nothing real compels you to think useless thoughts.

787. Real positive thinking is based on true and practical spiritual ideas.

788. True thoughts always bring with them a good feeling.

789. Thought-watching is a highly enjoyable and practical adventure.

THE PAIN EXPLAINED

790. Strain and pain are always wrong for you.

791. The pain is in the world in here, not out there.

792. You are in pain because you refuse friendly intelligence in favor of alien ignorance.

793. Most pain is unconscious.

794. My pain made me mean.

795. Make the pain get worse so you can see it. Let the pain get as bad as you can bear and then add to it.

796. When you learn the lesson in the pain, you will not have to repeat either the lesson or the pain.

797. The one thought that can break you out is this: It is not necessary for me to be in pain.

798. You think the absence of pain is the absence of you. But the absence of you is the absence of pain.

THE CURE

799. Truth is tough on pain. It is not tough on you.

800. I would be gloomy too if my mind worked like yours.

801. Don't expect heavenly soothing for your earthly stupidity.

802. I am going to start a brain-transplant business. May I count on you as a customer?

803. If you and your pain are the same thing, what can you do about it? You can do this. You can consciously refuse to do anything at all to relieve it. Don't phone your girlfriend to talk about it or be bitter because that man left you for another woman. What you can also do is understand that the slightest move towards removing the pain will keep it going. If you consciously refuse to do anything about the pain, that will increase the intensity. This intense watching is what increases the separation so that there is born in you something new that is not a part of emotional heartache. This is the beginning of

99

God, Truth, operating on the darkness inside of you. The light shining on the pain does the one thing that puts it away, which is to show you its actual nature. What it consists of is unseen movements passing through you that you in your non-evolvement say "I" to.

804. The cure is beautiful because it is close. It is as close as your willingness to hear and obey.

HEARTACHE CAN BE CONQUERED

805. Simply allow yourself to fall away from the sickness inside and outside. God will catch you.

806. *You* never break down. It's your misery that breaks down and you are not your misery.

807. When a problem comes, don't take it into yourself, but keep it at a distance.

808. Talk back consciously to what now defeats you. Say, "If you're so smart, how come I'm so miserable, so lost, so defeated, so wrong?" Already that's a bit of separation, standing apart from the miserable lower world and exposing it as something wrong for you.

809. Heartache can be conquered because a higher part of you is free and apart from heartache.

BE HONEST ABOUT YOUR CONDITION

810. There is no progress without first seeing your actual condition.

811. Two men were wandering around a dreary desert, lost and scared. One of them fell into a pit. The other fell into a gold mine. But both were still lost.

812. It is a miracle to see that you're trapped.

813. There is nothing so pleasant as honest misery. What a beautiful thing is honest misery. Do you understand that at all? The honesty that says, "I am nothing but a bundle of lies, of hatreds," that is a fact. And you know, even a negative fact is beautiful when seen.

814. Admit the truth of what you presently are and you admit the power of Heaven.

815. To overcome the devil, you must meet him but not deny that you're his, that you're completely lost. Say: "Feeling-that's-trying-to-take-me-over, I'm not going to accept your nature as being my nature anymore, as being necessary for me. I'm beginning to understand that I don't have to rely on you anymore for my feeling of life. That can't be life. There has to be Something Else!"

816. Your troubles are real only in the sense that you are still tormented by them, but they are not real in a higher sense. If you suffer by being lost in the hot and dry desert, you can learn how to escape the desert. Once you are out of the desert, the troubles of the desert no longer exist for you, though they still exist for those still lost in the desert.

IT'S YOUR WAY OR GOD'S WAY

817. The entire world is insisting on one thing: my way!

818. Work to see the difference between yielding to God and yielding to your own hardened neurosis.

819. Truth is definite.

820. Your problem is you can never be final about anything.

821. Truth cannot make a mistake.

822. Don't fear to know that all you are is a walking mistake.

823. Truth never argues with what is wrong.

824. You want your own way? You've got it.

825. The will of God is the life you can have. It is like a river, always flowing.

826. Count the cost.

827. You are unreal.

828. God is all that is real.

THE MIRACLE OF SILENCE

829. You find out who you are in silence. Go there by not trying to take your own thoughts with you.

830. It's okay to go silent. Nothing bad will happen to you.

831. The awakened state is a state of silence.

832. Only noise makes mistakes. Silence never makes mistakes.

833. Instead of becoming a little bit quiet, become totally quiet and see if the quietness is your friend or your foe.

834. You hope for a miracle in your life. It is possible for you to experience a real miracle. It happens when you hear your silence speak.

835. Go silent within yourself and wait on God.

REAL RESCUE

836. We can either hear what we want to hear or we can hear the rescuing truths.

837. Never, never, never rescue yourself. If you do you will have to go through the experience again.

838. While there is no you who can rescue you, there can be an impersonal awareness of the rescuing process. The rescue is complete when the awareness is complete.

839. Truth wants to rescue you.

840. You must take part in your own deliverance.

841. Who can be rescued? Whoever can still be sorry.

842. You will be rescued from yourself upon one condition. The condition is that you endure being called what you actually are inwardly. Rescue consists of going beyond your habitual and hostile reaction to being called what you actually are inwardly.

843. God is not going to enter your darkness. It is up to you to see where you're at in the slums and get out of there!

844. You are quite convinced that it is your doom to see that your self-glorified self cannot win but it is really your only rescue.

845. Wish right now to be genuinely rescued and you will be.

SEEK ONLY TRUTH

846. This school is the Cosmic College of the world. It is very high indeed.

847. If one man can know so can another.

848. Make a unique effort to get a unique result.

849. If the mountain disappears as a necessity to climb, the mountain climber also disappears as a necessity to exist.

850. To give up being someone who has to go higher is the going higher.

851. You have nothing to live for except God.

852. Seek only the high places and you will have everything.

INNER-WORK EXERCISES

WATCH YOUR WALK What liberty to walk through the world and be free of it and of yourself. Even your body feels better. As an exercise, you will walk in a new way. Watch your walk, especially how unnatural it is. Noticing of your unnaturalness is what begins to eliminate it.

THE BLANK SPACE Ask yourself, "What was I about to say?" Since you only read a wrong inner script, all the parts you read are wrong too. This exercise is designed to bring higher judgment down to the mechanical inner script to correct it. Go right into the new situation daring to have nothing to say. See the blank space yawn before you and don't rush in to fill it.

SIT BACK The cause and cure of your pain is in you. You keep it going by answering the world. For example, why do you answer an accusation from inside or outside you? You answer because you want to protect yourself. Why don't you just sit back and listen very attentively to what is being said and not do, say or feel anything in return. When you first start this you won't know what to do, which is the precise objective of it. You'll be scared and confused about what is going to happen to you. You always knew what to do before. You got nervous, rageful or passed it off as a joke. The demons inside you will try to force you to go into the grab bag of your usual responses because they know they are in danger. Do practice this very simple, very basic, workable and profound technique of sitting back.

KNOW THE MACHINE On a piece of paper write, "What I do when I am scared." Then list numerically what you do. Keep it simple. Write down everything you remember. This includes all the centers: physical, mental, emotional and the sex center. For example: 1. I get tense. 2. I get anxious. 3. I get jealous. 4. I retreat. The longer the list, the better work you are doing and the more you know about the machine. With that knowledge something higher than the machine will repair it for you.

• • •

Chapter 5
THE TRUTH ABOUT THIS WORLD

THIS WORLD IS NOT YOUR WORLD

853. You are really not a citizen of this world permanently. You see, you always forget that.

854. If you were meant for this world, this world would have made you happy.

855. Do you think God put you in this world without a way out?

856. Friendship with the world is enmity with God.

857. You can do what God wants you to do instead of what sick society wants you to do.

858. You can be in the world but not of it.

LIVE FROM YOUR TRUE NATURE

859. Society says, "We know what is best for you." That is a monstrous lie. You will get nothing from society. And yet we abandon our integrity and swallow it whole. No one knows what is best for you except the real you.

860. You must see the difference between the artificial needs of your false nature and the true needs of your True Nature.

861. See how you are always trying to protect your viewpoints, your attitudes, your way of life. You are trying desperately to protect it because it's all you've got. You lie and say, "This is all I can have." Why do you lie like that?

862. Where did you pick up all your present methods, values, procedures for living in this world? Well,

you had to pick them up from outside. You began to believe in this world. It is about time you found out that the world that insisted you believe in it is nothing but drudgery. They all lied to you and you didn't know it. Everyone bothering everyone else, everyone misleading everyone else.

863. If you want to know what it's like to feel good all the time, go from social solutions up to spiritual solutions.

864. You don't have to get hurt because you don't have to feel hurt. You don't have to feel hurt when there is no feeler there, no impostor-self saying, "Grab all you can, yell at the other person, get some advantage over someone else."

865. Living from your real nature is the same as doing something worthwhile with your life.

ONE GIANT MISTAKE

866. Consider very seriously the possibility that the human race has made a gigantic blunder. It is so gigantic that we don't even see it.

867. The failure of a human being to see the contradiction between what he says and what he is is the great destroyer of humanity.

868. The world is controlled by unconscious attitudes.

869. Man's ignorance and fear create the very conditions he cannot understand and which he fears.

870. The painful human contradiction is easily explained: A man behaves like a devil and then expects to be treated like an angel.

871. Evil and tricky people lead good but shallow people astray.

872. The trick is to make human beings feel guilty for standing up to evil.

873. Badness cannot invade us unless it has our permission to do so.

874. Let the following powerful fact swirl around in your mind. Let it go wherever it wants to go and reveal whatever it wants to reveal: *The world is one giant mistake!*

THIS WORLD HAS NOTHING OF REAL VALUE TO GIVE YOU

875. The world has nothing of real value to give you because it does not exist. Because it does not exist as a reality, because it is illusory, it has only illusory and worthless rewards for you. While employment and geography and people exist for your physical self and your social self and are good for them, they cannot give benefits to your real spiritual nature, which is complete in itself. It always has been complete and always will be for it lives not in time but in eternity.

In Reality there is no individual who can win a thrill or a sense of worthiness from the everyday world. In a lost person rewards or punishments from the world fall on the self-glorified self and cause it to vibrate. This vibration serves as a shaky idol which we eagerly worship for as long as the thrill lasts. But since the worshipper and his idol are the same thing, the same set of vibrations, the ending of the thrill of worshipping the idol causes self-panic. We feel as if we are fading away, that we will not be ourselves anymore. The fear of the extinction of the invented self prevents us from seeing that the false self must fade away in order to experience true spiritual birth.

Your work in all this is to notice the deceptive nature of your fear of not existing. And one way to do this is to notice how friends, news stories, rumors of doom, how they all try to plant fearful thoughts and feelings into your system. Here is what these people are doing: In order to give themselves a false sense of aliveness by making gloomy remarks they have no conscience in making others feel the same false sense of doom. They are like mad musicians who demand that you dance to their insane music. Everything in this paragraph connects with the opening sentence, which is: The world has nothing of real value to give you because it does not exist.

876. What is important to the world is not important to you. What is unimportant to the world is not unimportant to you.

MAKING SENSE OF HUMAN LIFE

877. Think from Truth about life, not from life about Truth.

878. Life cannot make sense on the level of life.

879. The world is wasting itself doing unnecessary things.

880. The entire world lives like seals performing before the audience, always looking for more applause.

881. Ridiculous—that is the word that best describes human beings.

882. All good gifts, all real values, come down from God.

883. You have not yet learned to value the invisible over the physical.

884. A beautiful technique for inner transformation is to ask yourself, "What is the spiritual thing to do?"

885. Try to read the newspaper from a spiritual viewpoint.

886. All of society lives from an endless deceptive practice. That practice is to perform the unnecessary and the harmful while trying to make them look like the necessary and the beneficial.

887. It is extremely dangerous to give people unearned benefits. It first destroys the receiver of unearned benefits, then it destroys the society that gives out unearned benefits. The givers destroy the receivers and themselves. It is an absolute spiritual law that every benefit in life must be individually earned.

888. Human life is nothing but nonsense surrounded by more nonsense surrounded by more nonsense.

889. Human existence on earth makes no sense at all the way it presently operates, so any effort you make to make sense out of it will only drive you more senseless. You cannot make sense out of ordinary human life, but you can understand clearly that it makes no sense. This places you on a high level which alone makes sense.

TOUGH STUFF THAT HEALS

890. Truth is the most unpopular product in the world. People say they want it but their lives prove otherwise.

891. God is the only thing in the universe that does not stop. Everything else comes to an end but God alone continues.

892. People go to vile places instead of staying home and trying to make contact with God.

893. The one question that will send dark human beings into a rage is to ask, "How long is it going to last?"

894. Rage is lunacy on the loose and a lunatic mind fights fiercely for its own preservation. It is like a

father devil who fanatically protects his young imps, for he needs to use them for his own evil purposes.

895. Do you feel better now that you have made that hateful accusation and told a lie as well?

896. In the early stages of growth the spiritual student will try to block these things out of his mind. He will not want to see them.

897. This is tough stuff, yes, but it is the tough stuff that heals you.

898. Self-healing is well underway when you are living from a constant, specific viewpoint toward the world. That viewpoint is, "You have nothing for me. I don't want anything you presently have."

899. Remember this and it will save you years of work: Nobody loves you but God.

RIGHT PRIORITIES

900. You can have everything in this earthly existence you need to obtain.

901. Serve your true interest, not your self-interest.

902. You don't have to try anymore to give importance to your life. You're not going to find it!

903. Inwardly you possess all you need.

904. False needs wear you out. You don't have to serve false needs anymore.

905. Whatever you do, be it mechanical work, whether you sell things for a living or just stay at home and take care of the children, you can do these things without looking for them to fulfill your inner self.

906. The throne that the emperor is on belongs to God.

907. Go ahead and participate in business. Go ahead and make the sales. But be free of the results. Whether you make the sale or don't make the sale, all day long you will work for something higher. Your attention will be on more important things.

908. Care for nothing except staying awake.

909. Misuse of attention is one of our greatest faults.

910. The only power wrongness has is the attention you give it.

911. Anytime you want, you can change your attention.

912. Attention must be in the right place at the right time.

913. Turn your attention toward something that is higher than your thinking patterns.

914. A tremendous secret of right action is to do one thing at a time and to know that you are doing it. When you do that, there cannot be any resentment over doing an unwanted task such as the dishes, for example. You do it because it has to be done.

WATCH OUT FOR DECEITFUL PEOPLE

915. Social life is a madhouse.

916. Human beings rush frantically around trying to prove they are right when they are wrong.

917. People are very much against evil providing it is the other person's evil.

918. The motto of every human being is: I want to be more important than you.

919. The virtues of most human beings are whatever their sickness says they are.

920. A deceitful coward proclaims, "We must discuss our problem." But a valorous person reflects, "I must

ponder my problem." There are many lessons in this, and here is one of them: Be alert to people who sneakily try to drag you into their swamps by using words such as *we* and *our* and *us*. Once you start struggling in the swamp, watch how quickly *our problem* is scornfully replaced by *your problem.*

921. Always remember that the world rewards its own. The more you lie and deceive people, the more you get from this world in position and power.

922. If a man is insane and two hundred million people claim he is sane, he is still insane.

THE TRUTH ABOUT SOCIETY

923. Society mauls everyone from the very second they are born.

924. Society is cunning, persistent and absolutely heartless in its attempts to turn the individual into its own maniacal nature.

925. The most tragic thing that can happen to a human being is to no longer want to know the difference between good and bad.

926. Human beings have allowed sickness to become their God.

927. The mentally sick substitute hatred for intelligence while, of course, hatefully denying that they do so.

928. Call my sickness health and I will love you. Call my sickness sickness and I will hate you.

929. Propaganda destroys the propagandist.

930. Remember these three facts: 1. Human beings are tricky and deceitful beyond description. 2. Hardly anyone sees this. 3. You must see it if you are going to break out.

931. A sure sign of spiritual growth is to see that it is a thousand times worse than you thought, both in this world and in you.

932. You run into one problem after another because you really don't realize that you live in an insane world. This insanity includes both the outer world and your own inner lunacy. Now this is not a cruel or insulting thing to say to you; in fact, it may be the first gift of compassion you have ever received in your entire life. Can you see why? You have been told how to end your problems once and for all. To review, you must clearly admit both exterior and interior insanity, which is the first daring step toward sanity and problem-free days.

YOU'RE ON THE SPIRITUAL BATTLEFIELD

933. You don't know that you're in a war. I want you to be on the winning side. Now you're not.

934. Underneath it all, the real battle is between God and Satan.

935. *You* can't win but there is winning for you.

936. This class will not destroy you by telling you comforting lies.

937. Every human being on earth is either wanting Satan to lose and God to win, or they're wanting Satan to win and God to lose.

938. I have forgotten something. I have not been fighting in the name of the King.

939. The battle is won only by risking and suffering wounds. But at the end of the victorious battle all wounds are healed.

940. Conscious ego-defeat is victory.

941. If we fight to keep our unlife we will never have True Life.

942. My defeat is God's victory.

943. You must make the right decision—to place yourself on the side of God. You must make the decision over and over again.

944. You will win because God has already won.

SATAN, SOCIETY AND YOUR SANITY

945. Satan loves to make people believe he doesn't exist. This is his first order of business.

946. Remember that Satan and insanity are the same thing.

947. There exists a sinister and worldwide conspiracy to drive you insane, for insane human beings can be enslaved with deceptive promises. Your chance for escaping insanity consists of understanding this fact instead of fearing it. And one fact you must understand is that you in your present state are a part of this maniacal conspiracy. All dark-minded human beings are part of it but do not know it. Remember the following guideline: the next time you feel helpless in the face of the world's insanity, discover who is the *who* who feels helpless.

948. Madness is to think that a cluster of thoughts is you.

949. Cowards crave crazy crowds.

950. Humans love panic.

951. People go crazy because it is a convenient defense against going sane.

952. A sane mind knows it was once crazy.

953. One characteristic of a sane mind is its refusal to

get involved in society's insanity because it recognizes insanity when it sees it.

954. Do everything possible to cooperate with God in favor of your sanity.

955. Sanity in the atmosphere strikes an insane mind as being odd and uncomfortable. The strangeness forces it to try to switch the atmosphere over to its own insane nature. But since this is impossible, the insane mind turns hateful toward the sanity and also, of course, falls into self-torment.

LOST PEOPLE

956. The world is lost because the individual is lost.

957. Lostness does not know it is lost, which is why a lost person has neither understanding nor interest in his lost condition. Only awareness of his lostness can arouse a person toward finding himself.

958. The angry and fearful reaction of lost people when you tell them they are lost is perfect proof they are lost.

959. In its twisted logic the false self feels perfectly justified in destroying, for it believes that its existence depends upon having enemies. When destroying a self-created enemy, it can then lie to itself and excitedly exclaim, "See, someone was destroyed; therefore, a destroyer must exist—me! Thank heaven, I am a destroyer and not a nobody." But it cannot really convince itself that its lie is a truth. This is its daily agony.

960. A lost human being doesn't care if he wrecks the whole world as long as he feels the sick pleasure in the wrecking.

961. Remember always that other people will do everything they can to prevent you from breaking out.

962. When someone demands proof of the rightness of these higher teachings you can be sure that nothing will be accepted as proof by him. Proof, which is an inner revelation, is the last thing he wants for it would destroy what he values most—his pleasure of poisoning himself.

963. It is the dedicated duty of every lost human being to keep you as lost as he is.

964. The sick stick thick.

965. Just remain true and watch how easy it is to ignore the demands of lost people.

SEE THE WORLD BY SEEING YOURSELF

966. To rise above this world you must see the actual condition of this world.

967. This world is on the Titanic.

968. See the world as it is by seeing yourself as you are.

969. The world out there and the world in here are the exact same world. Both are one and the same criminal gang.

970. There are no social problems, only individual problems.

971. Human beings don't want to see that their boat is sinking. They go back and tell the orchestra to play another dance.

972. The angels of Heaven rejoice when a human being admits how bad off inside he really is.

973. If I yearn to be accepted by a sick society, what does that tell me about myself?

974. The reason you should expose your sickness is that sickness has no future.

975. You still want something from man instead of everything from God.

STOP BEING SO GULLIBLE

976. The more you let other people tell you how to sail your boat, the less the boat belongs to you.

977. Dark forces cannot exist without ignorant gullibility.

978. Write down the word *gullibility*. Look it up in the dictionary. Study it.

979. Human beings fall off the cliff because they are so gullible.

980. Stop depending on an undependable world.

981. When you don't have the solid answers from yourself you'll ask anyone, which is folly because you can think for yourself. When you begin to think, know, decide, live from yourself, your life willchange. So study yourself very carefully for daily evidences that you are asking people to think for you. See for yourself that you don't think for yourself. If you did, you'd never ask anyone for approval, which can only be approval of your wrong nature.

Now see how gullible you are so you can use shocks to dissolve shocks. You do have a helper— Truth, something that will come to you upon the invitation of your sincerity. Observe Truth working on you, rebuking bad parts and encouraging right parts. Ask Truth to reveal your foolishness to you. After the storm comes the rainbow. So go through it and get beyond the urge and compulsion to let someone else think for you. Submit to the tutelage of Truth!

982. When you have rightly explained yourself to yourself no one will ever be able to trick you into a wrong self-explanation.

DON'T ASK ANYONE FOR ANYTHING

983. Satan threatens people by saying that if you follow me, I will give you the rewards of this world. And if you don't follow me, I will not give you the rewards of this world.

984. One of the main reasons you don't change is that you refuse to see that all packages delivered to you by human beings, including yourself, are empty.

985. Human sickness can never be satisfied with what it demands and gets. It feels a short thrill over winning its demands, after which it restlessly returns to demand more for itself.

986. Satan makes sure that the wrong way looks pretty.

987. You can work for time or eternity.

988. Any person taking a paycheck from Satan always dreads the next paycheck.

989. Don't ask anyone for anything. Don't plead with anyone for companionship, sex, approval.

990. Self-centered sociality is enmity against God and man.

991. Spiritual unfoldment is really an increasing awareness of what you can do without.

NO MORE HEROES

992. All heroes are accidental.

993. Admiration is a terrible thing. It is division. Admiring God or someone else means you are apart. The idea stands between you and the good life.

994. You need not idolize or yearn for anyone. But you must see very deeply into this in order to discover your basic error. You really do not admire that man or love that woman. Unknowingly, you

admire and love your own thoughts and feelings about them. Having imitation strength and beauty inside yourself, you project them outwardly and then deceive yourself into thinking that they reside inside that man or woman. You will get an endless series of pains and disappointments as long as you unconsciously approve of this kind of self-trickery.

995. I'm trying to destroy all your human heroes. But you won't let me. You still want to be one yourself.

996. Anytime you want to be the big hero, you are going to be awfully nervous about it.

997. The intellect angrily fears its dismissal as the hero of the universe. The very knowledge of this helps you to get on with its dismissal, which makes you sane and happy.

998. No more human heroes! Love the Creator, not the creation.

SEE THROUGH DISGUISES

999. When looking at someone, have you ever suspected that there is another person hiding behind the person you see out front? Your suspicion is correct.

1000. Study humans who seek to appear powerful and authoritative and connect them with ghosts who are supposed to look scary, appearing to be light and having life. Light however dissipates ghosts, reveals them as being nothing, which they always were.

1001. Switching personalities wears you out.

1002. A sense of humor indicates at least a small degree of separation from the falsely serious thought-self. Now ponder this next idea: Professional comedians are the last people to have a real sense of humor.

1003. So-called "spiritual" people can't be light-hearted because they must be on guard.

1004. Society is like a crowd in carnival costumes with everyone fearful that others will see through his disguise.

1005. It is possible to see how idiotic and foolish human beings are without feeling superior to them. As an exercise, list human types you have observed or known.

A NEW KIND OF SUCCESS

1006. At the end of the day you have to account for how you spent it. How did you spend it? Did you notice that you believed in the social system because you thought it could reward you?

1007. Every time you try to conquer the world, the world conquers you.

1008. If you use your intellect and emotions against the world, you're going to get mauled.

1009. You keep asking how to succeed. Here is one way: Become active to the higher, passive to the lower.

1010. When you do your work, do it well, whatever it is. But don't desire to be a success in the eyes of society.

1011. Life-victory arrives by desiring spiritual answers more than you desire exterior results.

1012. Winning in this world is nothing but a thought and a feeling. Losing in this world is nothing but a thought and a feeling.

1013. Stop helping your captors—your unconscious feelings and thoughts.

1014. A false man loses even when he appears to win. A true man wins even when he appears to lose.

1015. Spiritual success starts when weariness with not winning is replaced by weariness with not understanding.

HOW TO HANDLE BAD BEHAVIOR

1016. The world pleasantly pleads, "Please cooperate with my sickness." If you refuse, the smile is replaced by hatred.

1017. A sick mind loves pain.

1018. Gloom is passive instability; insolence is active instability.

1019. When you see someone who is unable to remain quiet, you are seeing a sick human being.

1020. There is one absolute and unbreakable sign by which you can know a sicko when you see one. When something goes wrong with him, it is always the fault of someone else.

1021. The sicko's creed: "I want the privilege of wrecking my life and I want it to be your privilege to straighten it out."

1022. Sickies take their courage from other sickies.

1023. A sicko is very grateful to another sicko who gives him something to be sick about. For example, a rude person eagerly awaits another rude person's sarcastic remark, after which they fight with grateful enjoyment and destruction.

1024. Kindness and generosity can never help a sick human being who has already made up his mind to remain sick. He will take everything he can get from you but he has no intention of changing inwardly.

1025. Never show weak politeness toward a sicko. He will sense it as fearful cowardice on your part, which it surely is. You need only one perfect rule for dealing with a sicko: Let your words and your manner reveal inner strength.

DON'T FIGHT THIS WORLD

1026. This sentence should be enough for you to study for the next year: Study instead of fight.

1027. Unconsciously you create things to fight.

1028. You don't have to fight this world. You just have to get out of it.

1029. Stop fighting your desolation and emptiness.

1030. Anything you fight, you create.

1031. When you fight, you are a slave.

1032. A right aim is to refuse absolutely to ever attack anyone or anything again.

1033. You've been defending something that doesn't exist.

1034. Fighting is false fun.

1035. When a hostile person demands an explanation of a spiritual truth, he really does not want an explanation. He just wants to be given ammunition he can fire back at you. No matter what answer he is given, his spirit of hatred is ready to tear it apart. Such a person is a devil so you should wisely and calmly treat him like one. Happily, your own spiritually mature nature will effortlessly handle him for you. Never argue or discuss Truth with this kind of person. To do so is to descend to his loathsome level.

1036. Let the fighter and the world being fought collapse.

1037. Let yourself be defeated. Let all your friends leave you. Don't get the new home. Don't be popular.

Lose everything, including the wish to fight for yourself in the wrong way.

1038. Half your conflicts will end by realizing that you cannot hold in your hand both a sugary lollipop and a healthy loaf of bread. It is one or the other. So hear is a new class poem for you to memorize: Drop, drop the lollipop.

1039. When you are at the mercy of anyone or anything and do not fight, you have won.

1040. Fighting inner darkness in the wrong way is the same as submitting to it. Truth will show you how to truly fight for Light.

SEE THE INSANITY OF THIS WORLD

1041. This is a sleeping, thief-in-the-night world.

1042. Samson was clipped when he let Delilah put him to sleep.

1043. Like other products, music comes in many varieties and qualities. There is pretty music, healthy music, boring music, sentimental music and there is insane music. Listen carefully and you will hear shrieks of human despair concealed in sick music.

1044. I am going to give you some very shocking facts about human evil. Creatures from hell are right here in this world. Let what I am going to tell you sink in deeply. Pernicious propaganda is being imposed on you in many different ways, through whomever you meet. Everyone wants to believe in themselves by fooling you. So remember these facts. Sickness hates health and wants to destroy it. Badness considers goodness an enemy to be persecuted. Misery wants to harm happiness. The sneaky man has contempt for an honest man.

Dirtiness hates cleanness and tries to turn cleanness into dirtiness. Darkness despises Light.

1045. Watch the news and imagine the TV screen is a window into a lunatic asylum because it is. Watch the expression on those people's faces, the increasing dirtiness and crudeness right in front of your eyes. Feel rightly repelled by this evil world. When you're altogether repelled, you'll never be depressed again because the last thing you'll want is its favors. You'll want to get away from it as fast as you can and stay away from it.

1046. Lose confidence in this world without feeling bitter, critical or hateful toward it.

1047. When you see the horror of the world, make an effort to wake up and stay awake.

1048. The world is simply an immense insane asylum and there is no difference between the patients and the doctors.

CATCH THE REAL THIEF

1049. The psychological and physical criminals of society all say the same thing: "You did it to me, now it's my turn to do it to you."

1050. When you complain about anything, that anything that you are complaining about is you yourself. You think it is out there, the way that person treated you. You say, "Look what they have done to me!" That is the storm. It comes from the false way you think, from your undeveloped emotions, from your childish reactions. If you haven't gotten to the point in your inner journey yet where you know that you curse the whole world, you are going to have to go through disappointment after disappointment.

1051. Only the tough stuff is going to do it. Only the blunt facts. And here is one: Everyone wants to live off of everyone else.

1052. Human beings have nothing. Think of a mountain with 10,000 caves. Everyone is looking into each other's dark and empty cave to see if there is something they can steal. This is the way it is. Human beings think they can get something from other human beings who are as sick and empty as they are.

1053. Con men always stun you. That way they throw you out of your reasoning faculties.

1054. One evil loves to pounce upon another evil in an effort to trick people into thinking that it is not evil. It usually works because foolish human beings automatically believe that only goodness denounces evil. It seldom occurs to the limited thinking of most people that evil delights in condemning evil.

1055. People are so sick in their minds that they do not know they are sick in their minds.

1056. Anyone who lacks plain and simple good manners in public is an animal disguised as a human being. And that is not too strong a description.

1057. The behavior of a vicious person is the perfect proof of the truth of everything you are reading.

1058. People who have physical violence are asking for it.

1059. When you permit someone to drain your energy, to steal your time, you are committing a crime against yourself and I order you to stop it now.

1060. Here is something that is impossible: It is impossible to explain to one devil-dominated human being that another devil-dominated human being is devil-dominated.

1061. What the spiritual criminal does is deliver hell while promising heaven.

1062. The world is destroyed by *good* people.

1063. Is there no end to the cruelty of human beings causing fear and misery to other human beings? No, there is absolutely no end to it. Only you can stop causing fear and misery.

DON'T GIVE IN TO WRONG DEMANDS

1064. When a frantic world tries to carry you away, remind yourself that you need not go.

1065. Anytime you wish to be relieved of false responsibilities and compulsive duties, remember this: You owe everything to Reality and nothing to humanity.

1066. Dear society, don't tell me what I want. I will tell myself what I want.

1067. Each man has all the wisdom of the world in himself.

1068. For the sake of rightness, you must learn to disappoint others and yourself.

1069. Get off the stage and you will have no fear of non-applause from the audience.

1070. The difference between living under your own power and under the power of social influence is the difference between songs and tears.

1071. The next time you get an unasked for gift, I want you to be under no obligation to give them one in return. You politely thank them and that is it.

1072. When someone pokes and pries into your life, say inwardly, and outwardly if necessary, "I don't wish to explain." After bearing it consciously and nervously for the first fifty times, the trembling will begin to fade away the fifty-first time.

1073. Don't give neurotic people a reward. When you permit them to upset you, you are giving them a reward.

1074. Anyone who tries to talk reason with an insane mind is insane himself. There is just one sane thing to say to an insane person. That one thing is, "Goodbye."

1075. When you see someone crying, run away fast. The guiltier you feel, the faster you should run.

1076. Neurotic people will always try to convince you that their problems are your problems. Don't listen.

1077. Politely do what is right and endure the other person's negative reaction.

1078. Be tactful in this world. Don't kick a sleeping tiger.

1079. Silence in the face of an accusation leaves the problem where it belongs—with the accuser.

1080. Make a contribution to the world—Wake Up!

COME OUT FROM AMONG THEM

1081. There is one thought, one supreme truth, that society is adamantly against and doesn't at all want you to hear. That truth is: *The damage can be undone.*

1082. How do you get through to a world full of people selling their souls for the applause of their fellow lunatics?

1083. An insane world does not know that it is insane and when you tell it that it is insane, its reaction proves both its insanity and its inability to see the fact.

1084. The one thing for which people will never forgive you is for you to tell them the truth about themselves.

1085. Tell a man how to save a few dollars and he'll love you. Tell him how to save his soul and he will hate you.

1086. You have been called to "Come out from among them."

1087. God put you here to save yourself, not the world.

YOUR BRIGHT FUTURE IN THE REAL WORLD

1088. Always keep a glowing light in your mind, such as this: I only can enjoy my own recovered spiritual nature.

1089. If you can see in the dark, is there darkness for you?

1090. Almost the entire world is submitting to dark forces. They are submitting for protection, not seeing that they are being destroyed.

1091. Human beings are walking in a dark room, bumping into each other and remarking how nice it is to live in the light.

1092. A warring world has no power to injure your real nature anymore than darkness can shake a tree.

1093. Let Light come to you and penetrate into the dark recessed areas of your mind. Let Truth enter.

1094. Your inner eyes can see the invisible spiritual world.

1095. The inner world is the only real life that exists.

1096. If the horrible world which exists outside you does not also exist inside you, it is the same for you as if it does not exist outside you.

1097. When the world is not in you, the world cannot scare you.

1098. You owe nothing to darkness, to evil. Christ said, "My Kingdom is not of this world."

1099. Brightness is from Truth alone. It comes from living within the Kingdom.

1100. There is another world and it exists for you to live in and enjoy.

INNER-WORK EXERCISES

READ The next time you pick up anything to read, know that you picked it up.

FACE THE FACES Watch how influenced you are by facial expressions. Catch as many as you can as often as you can every day. Say to yourself, "That severe look has bluffed me for the last time."

DETACHMENT Begin to practice detachment from the event. Practice watching clearly an event in your life—an unkind remark, for instance—and see how you are driven frantic trying to do something with it. Watch the urging to answer with a snappy, sarcastic remark. Begin to see that something of which you are unaware is living your life for you and that it will continue until you start to work.

A MESSAGE TO YOURSELF Write down the following sentence and carry it with you for a week: *There is no one there and there is nothing to fight.*

• • •

Chapter 6
COMMAND LIFE

LET TRUTH TELL YOU WHAT TO DO

1101. There is only one tyrant in life, which is a lack of understanding of life. Since understanding can be acquired, the tyrant need not be endured.

1102. Inner light shows you what to do with yourself all day long, making everything comfortable.

1103. To understand life, all you need to do is study what comes your way. See it and let revelation come to you.

1104. The *you* is the suffering victim of people and circumstances. The *un-you* is the peaceful commander of people and circumstances.

1105. Things are going to turn up as you are, not as you want.

1106. Right action is to see that no action is needed.

1107. The only real mistake in any experience is the neglect to use the experience to release more inner light.

1108. The old nature must go.

1109. I know what to do. I will relax and let the Spirit enter and clear the junk away from me.

1110. Your true nature never needs to anxiously prove itself to others but lives in calm command like a popular king.

THE DELUSION OF CONTROL

1111. To gain control of your life, you must first lose your thousands of delusions that you already have control. But these delusions will lie to you frantically and cunningly to prevent you from seeing them as false control. Losing control in the right way means to see that you never ever had control in the first place. This is a part of inner awakening. It is like having a nightmare of being chased by ghosts but upon awakening in the morning, you gain complete control over the ghosts by seeing their nothingness.

1112. You don't make choices—they make you. Catch yourself saying, "What should I do?" And ask yourself, "Who is asking the question?" Who is asking the question is a very apprehensive so-called *you* inside that wants to perpetuate itself in needing to go this way or that.

1113. It is pure delusion that you make your own intelligent decisions. All you do is to eagerly follow the dominating self-desire of the moment. Know that there is such a life as a choiceless life which has no contradiction. It comes to anyone who admits to the myth of having independent judgment and choice.

1114. You control nothing and you don't have to.

1115. If anyone wants to be the boss, always let him be the boss. You have no need to be in charge. What do you need to be in charge of? You're in charge of yourself.

1116. Give up all control and you will have control.

BE WILLING TO BE WRONG

1117. You really have only one problem—you refuse all the clear evidence that you are wrong. Change all that. Just now the most important thing you can be is to be wrong. Be as fearful as you like of being wrong but be wrong. Just be wrong. It is not wrong to be wrong; it is right to be wrong. And it is also healthy and liberating.

1118. Wrongness *feels* wrong. If you understood this, this one statement could lead you all the way out of the jungle.

1119. The hoax was played on you and on me so subtly, so carefully and so persistently that you didn't know what was happening to you. And finally, when you woke up one morning with the heartache, with that tragedy, with that mess in your life, with that pain, with that anxiety, with that worry, then it dawned on you that something was seriously wrong with you, with you personally. Don't you dare shift the blame to anyone else. You are responsible for breaking the hoax that was imposed on you.

1120. The person who causes the grief is the one who suffers from it and the one who has to correct it.

1121. Who has all these troubles? The wrong way your mind operates.

1122. William can never tell William what is right.

1123. Don't take explanation as condemnation.

1124. The saddest words of tongue or pen: There's no use trying to correct him because he will just get mad.

1125. I don't know a more relieving statement than "I don't know."

1126. Be willing to be wrong.

1127. Each time you admit to yourself that you were wrong about something, you become right about something and instantly win the resulting reward.

1128. The three steps to spiritual wholeness: 1. A man is wrong while imagining he is right. 2. A man is wrong and knows he is wrong. 3. A man is right and knows he is right.

LIFT YOUR BURDENS

1129. One lesson well-learned can lift a thousand burdens.

1130. You grow healthier as you less and less hide things about yourself from yourself.

1131. Think of the power of this one sentence and what it could do for you if you understood it: You fear the loss of your distress.

1132. If I had a jar of pink pills here and I said, "Ladies and gentlemen, here's a free pink pill. All you have to do is swallow it and all your pains, all your heartaches, all your problems will vanish," none of you would take it. You'd be afraid to take it because you would ask me, "Who would I be after I got rid of my pain?"

1133. A nonexistent person is worrying that he will stop existing.

1134. Relief always comes from throwing away nonsense.

TRUE INTELLIGENCE CAN BE YOURS

1135. You are not required to be brilliant or wise. That comes later. You are required to just be honest.

1136. Stupidity hurts, while intelligence does not hurt. Examining this fact, how intelligent are you?

1137. There's no intelligence in anger. There's no intelligence in worry. There's no intelligence in being depressed. There's no intelligence in being hostile. There's no intelligence whatever in thinking about yourself because there's no self there to think about.

1138. Stupidity consists of not seeing the danger you are to yourself and others.

1139. It is intelligent to see that there is no self to be called dumb.

1140. When you no longer need to prove your intelligence, you have it.

1141. Good is always smarter than evil.

1142. Why don't you let every man-made, woman-made, self-made theory and scheme collapse and let God enter your life and let God be your intelligence?

END FEAR FOREVER

1143. Is your fear worth the price you pay to keep it?

1144. You have no business fearing anyone.

1145. The love of being afraid is one of the greatest enemies of mankind.

1146. You picked up the habit of being scared from every human being you have ever met.

1147. Fear is simply a hardened habit.

1148. The phrase that is constantly going on down deep in your psychology is: Please don't get mad at me.

1149. The only thing you fear is your own weakness.

1150. Think of what scares you now. It will not scare you when you allow the beautiful, marvelous Truth to be your life.

1151. Fear has no choice but to leave you if you follow the spiritual rules.

1152. I am not going to cringe before life which does not mean I am going to be hostile.

1153. One day you will look calmly at a fear and say to it, "You have shaken me for the last time."

DARE TO DO MORE

1154. You can have a life of stimulation or you can have a life of inspiration.

1155. Inner-work attracts right feelings from on high.

1156. You are never asked whether you are able to do a particular bit of spiritual work. You are just asked to do it.

1157. The more we dare do, the more we can do.

1158. You have to get more scared, more ashamed, more whatever. Let more work fall upon you than you can bear.

1159. When I go against myself, I go for myself.

1160. You can work in spite of your own laziness. You can work in spite of your own hatred. You can work in spite of that person who might be displeased with you. *IN SPITE OF* is magic.

1161. Always do what you don't want to do. That's the secret.

WELCOME HEALING SHOCKS

1162. God doesn't need your help.

1163. Anything that upsets us is a friend, not an enemy.

1164. Dark forces want to take away from you the ability to be shocked. The ability to be shocked is a spiritual talent. Develop it to the fullest.

1165. Our sickness has jolted us all these years. Now is the time to give it a jolt. Jolt it into oblivion.

1166. The tormenting feeling of hopelessness exists only in a person who still thinks he must be who he thinks he must be. The agony of hopelessness falls away from anyone who really sees that he need not be anyone at all in the eyes of himself or the world. Then hopelessness is replaced by living with complete power and peace, a new kind of power, a new kind of peace.

1167. You had better pray for the day—and some of you have had it—when you meet such a shocking experience that it shocks the nonsense and shocks the game out of you once and for all.

1168. Whatever can shock us can also heal us.

WIN BY LOSING

1169. Solutions are as close as your willingness to listen and obey Truth.

1170. You gain through loss.

1171. Dear God, show me how to get rid of the trash I have called treasure.

1172. You lose nothing when you lose your reputation, for you are not your reputation.

1173. Worry over losing the lower prevents winning the higher.

1174. You have an unconscious need to keep your petty little world in place.

1175. Other people are judging nothing real when they judge you.

1176. The world is out to get you all right, but if you are not the you the world thinks you are, it cannot get you.

1177. Total defeat is victory.

1178. Only when you finally confess that you cannot win in *your* way will you start to win in *the* way.

SLOW DOWN

1179. Where on earth are you rushing to?

1180. Any place your intellect takes you will be wrong.

1181. Relaxation means receptivity.

1182. Slow down, relax, be alert.

1183. Make small conscious decisions such as choosing to pick up the salt first and salting your food consciously. This is a good exercise which will slow you down.

1184. Esoterically, slowing down is rushing forward.

END PAINFUL COMPARISION

1185. What an odd kind of intelligence you have. It reveals itself only when it can compare itself with a stupid person. And notice how it never has trouble finding people who are stupid when compared with its supreme intelligence. As I said, what a peculiar kind of intelligence you have. It must depend upon another person—it cannot stand alone.

1186. See how your mind goes wrong regarding human relations. Notice your habit of instantaneously comparing yourself with everyone you meet.

1187. Comparison is the essence of sickness.

1188. We assemble with those we resemble.

1189. You hang around people like you because there is no upsetting comparision.

1190. You know you don't like yourself. Liking and disliking are both part of the false self in you. See that you've only made a big circle in the jungle. Where have you gone? Right back to yourself. So away with all comparison. It starts with you. It can end with you.

SELF-OBSERVATION

1191. Self-observation reveals. What follows after heals.

1192. The next time you pretend to not see wrongness in yourself, notice how your evasion nags and punishes you. Your noticing is an example of how the devil's pain can be used against him; that is, your insight into painful self-deception weakens its hold on you.

1193. When you really see that you are doing something against yourself, you will no longer do it.

1194. You will be aware when your wish to be aware is stronger than your wish to be unaware.

1195. The passive watcher has no problems.

SELF-DECEPTION

1196. The most heartless fiend on earth is named Aggressive Ignorance.

1197. Calling a foolish act a wise necessity is one of our more malicious and stubborn self-deceptions.

1198. Your ability to be told will grow equally as fast as your awareness that you cannot be told. Remember always, when you cannot be told, you do not realize that you cannot be told.

1199. I have found a magic formula for proving that I am always right. All I need do is to say that you are wrong.

1200. Self-deception is always unconscious.

1201. You are living in harmful self-deception if you get nervous or resentful when told you are living in harmful self-deception.

1202. The fact that you do not know is not your main problem. The fact that you do not know that you do not know is not your main problem. Your chief difficulty is that you do not know that you do not know and that a hostile spirit in you insists that things remain as they are. How weird and how pitiful. You worship your own ignorance.

1203. Your fiery desire is unable to put itself into another person's place for it recognizes no place but its own. This is an example of conceited self-destruction at its worst.

1204. Self-honesty heals self-deceit.

EXPOSE SELF-DOUBT

1205. You can live with a confidence that does not come from your mind at all.

1206. When do doubts enter? About ten seconds after you have proven that you are right.

1207. The weasel of self-doubt is always after you, especially after you have had a success.

1208. Do you know what hell is among other things? It's the five minutes following flattery.

1209. When a lost human being gets what he demands, he experiences these feelings in the following order: 1. Elation and ego-created cheerfulness. 2. The fading of elation and the entrance of small doubts about himself. 3. Increasing confusion and anxiety. 4. The desperate invention of a new demand in a useless attempt to quiet the haunting doubts.

1210. There are a thousand ways the devil can make Tom or Helen shake with doubt. There is no way the devil can make the true wisdom in Tom or Helen shake with doubt.

1211. The only way to get rid of self-doubt is to have no self there to doubt.

NEGATIVE EMOTIONS ARE UNNECESSARY

1212. The first step out of any negative state is to know you are in it.

1213. Always remember that negative emotions will present themselves as something good for you.

1214. If you did not take pleasure in anger, you would not be angry about anything. There is a great sick pleasure and ego-excitement in the thrill of hating or any other negative emotion.

1215. Fearful emotions are incapable of hearing anything outside of their own noise.

1216. Emotions are an exploding pool. Thought is a passive pond.

1217. Revenge is an explosion of mental dynamite.

1218. You can play with your toys of agitation and pretense, feeling that someone else is going to take care of you. When are you going to abandon infantile ways of living?

1219. The false nature will tell you that agitation is necessary for your survival.

1220. Try to find out who your closest negative buddy is, such as self-pity, bitterness, etc.

1221. The most sickening self-feeling of all is the self-feeling of self-sympathy.

1222. The next time you catch yourself falling into despair or any other negative emotion, negative thought or anything negative, you have to quietly say *NO* to it. You are to do this not once a day, not fifty times a day, but 500 times a day.

1223. Someday God will purify your emotions and they will be as pure as snow.

NATURALNESS

1224. You can live your day in an outflowing expression of natural energy.

1225. Be pleasantly touched by the following statement: There is no natural need for you to be bad.

1226. This will save you from so much false morality and false guidance: When you *do* better than you *are*, the doing is burdensome.

1227. All your life you run around trying to be like someone else. Why don't you try sometime being like yourself?

1228. You treat others exactly the way you treat yourself.

1229. Naturalness is common courtesy.

1230. All imitation is a burden. Mimicry is sad. Catch the strain and lack of naturalness in being an imitator and the uncertainty over whom to imitate. To leave the desert, cease following all human beings. Just be lost right in the middle of it all until all that is left in your life is complete despair, complete hopelessness. Note how you're following false guides, unnatural ways out. Despair is great as long as that's all there is. But you always seek a way out. Simply collapse right in the middle of the emptiness with no hopes at all and don't fear this state. Go for one small victory a day, a small bearing of your loneliness with no attempt to end it. This is ending it!

1231. Naturalness contains nothing of the usual kind of human goodness or badness, being neither a hawk nor a dove but only flight itself.

SOAR ABOVE YOUR TROUBLES

1232. You can fly as high as you want to fly.

1233. To be a flyer, just hear the higher.

1234. All our lives we have excused ourselves. There is no excuse whatever for any one of you now reading these words to not find yourself. That means there is no excuse for you loving your pain anymore because an alternative has been supplied. I am telling you that an alternative has been supplied and it is ready for your investigation and taking.

1235. You can't use a dark thought to chase out a dark thought.

1236. When I fiercely declare, "No one will ever hurt me again," I am already doing to myself what I don't want others to do.

1237. You are excusing yourself all the way into the dark depths of the bat cave.

1238. Thoughts go out and seek what is identical to them.

1239. Bats hate the light. They love darkness because it matches their own nature, which means they love themselves. Therefore it follows that bats must hate the light because it is unlike their own nature.

1240. Fly out of the bat cave.

1241. Like an eagle, your mind was created to soar.

PONDER THESE THINGS

1242. There is great wisdom in asking, "How can I get out of this?" There is even greater wisdom in asking, "How did I get into this?"

1243. Have you ever questioned how you live your life from hour to hour?

1244. A hoax is being played on me. What is it?

1245. Ask, "Could I be serving sickness without realizing it?"

1246. Use this sentence: "Just a minute, whose life is this?"

1247. The next time you feeled pushed around by life, ask who is the pusher and who is the pushed?

1248. Ask yourself, "Do I really want this self-destructive state?"

1249. The relief you really want is relief from yourself. But how can you have it when your whole life is dedicated to self-clinging?

1250. If understanding is conquest, how much further do you have to go to victory?

SIMPLE AND POWERFUL TRUTHS

1251. Remove ignorance, Truth dawns.

1252. To a bat, sunshine is bad news.

1253. I am not yesterday.

1254. There is no one there to make it.

1255. The damage can be undone.

1256. Live with uncertainty.

1257. Stay undecided.

1258. Wrongness is powerless.

1259. Inner change is all that counts.

1260. Directionless desire destroys discernment.

1261. You have to get used to being sane.

1262. Innocence is untouchable.

1263. All you need to be is a simple, good, decent human being.

1264. The Truth feels good.

FROM SELF-RIGHTEOUSNESS TO RIGHTNESS

1265. Human beings are compulsive chronic critics.

1266. Self-righteousness loves to be hypocritically shocked at the behavior of others.

1267. Conscious evaluation is not the same as criticism.

1268. I will give you a guaranteed method for keeping yourself dull and dejected. Just find pleasure in another person's real or imaginary mistake.

1269. The next time you condemn someone for something, look to see whether you might be more jealous than righteous.

1270. There is a simple test by which anyone can determine the depth of his own evil. His evil will equal the eagerness with which he detects and denounces evil in others.

1271. Self-development begins where self-righteousness ends.

1272. Dangerous delusions can be dissolved by the following method: Each time you catch someone in a mistake and feel delighted, catch yourself in a mistake and feel humiliated.

VICTORY OVER CIRCUMSTANCES

1273. We are not victims of circumstances because the circumstances are in us.

1274. It is impossible for any fact or circumstance to harm you, for the fact itself has neither punishment nor reward for your spiritual nature. Punishment comes only to false beliefs about yourself. It is when these false beliefs meet the fact and try to twist it for ego-serving motives that the damage occurs. The fact itself remains pure and innocent. For example, suppose you lose someone or something. That is the plain fact. Since your spiritual nature is complete and healthy, the idea of loss has no meaning to it. The lesson? Stick with the pure fact, and never descend into ego-serving interpretations of the fact.

1275. I am attributing power out there because I am falsely attributing power to my negative self, which doesn't exist.

1276. Remember the phrase, "Intelligent emptiness."

1277. If you're involved with someone who's hurting you by insisting upon being the boss, how does he get that power except by your stupid cooperation and remaining in the psychological and physical position where he can impose his demands on you? So who's at fault if you're under the tyranny of any other human being?

1278. The only proof is self-proof. Find some wrong, emotionalized state inside yourself and practice not being that. Watch what will happen to you as a result of no longer crying over anything, including the hideous injustice of this world. Everyone complains, everyone feels he's a victim. To live outside yourself you can never live for complaining, for revenge. You're going to have to just open your hands, let your life slip away and enter a horrible, terrifying emptiness—and just stay there.

1279. When I am my emptiness, Truth is my fullness.

1280. If I am not a victim of myself, I cannot be a victim of the world.

1281. During any tragedy say, "The best I understand it, I will put God first."

AWARENESS GIVES STRENGTH

1282. Your awareness that you're in the fog, that is the friend, that is the glow from Heaven, to know that you are absolutely helpless. You know just one thing, which is true intelligence. You know that all is wrong.

1283. An unaware man is unaware that he is unaware, therefore it has no meaning when you tell him he is unaware. Try explaining to a goat that he is unaware that he is a goat.

1284. You cannot think and be aware at the same time.

1285. The main danger is unawareness of danger. You have an ongoing warning system inside of you that is trying to tell you there are dangers around every corner, which there are.

1286. Dear God, help me to see that sick thought that just went through my mind as I walked across the living room.

1287. The awareness of weakness is the same as strength.

WHEN YOU DON'T KNOW WHAT TO DO

1288. When you don't know what to do, the only thing to do is to see fully that you don't know what to do and stop right there.

1289. Human beings are afraid they will one day run out of their self-induced experiences.

1290. When you know how to do it, you can cry your way all the way to dry eyes. Here is how to do it. See that tears are an admission of a total breakdown of your fraudulent solutions to your crisis. Realize just that much. Realize that you don't know what to do and never have. Remain with the emptiness experienced in the tears themselves. Stick with that. Now watch what happens next.

1291. When you don't know what to do, do nothing, for that is something.

1292. The grass grows all by itself, the birds fly all by themselves because God, the Great Caretaker of the universe, is taking care of the sparrows, taking care of the trees and the streams. God wanted to take care of you but you wouldn't let Him. You wanted to take care of yourself and look at the mess you've made! God will take care of the real you. He can't take care of the false you because there's really nothing there to take care of. You think there is. God thinks differently from you. The Great Caretaker right now wants you to understand, go into action and apply everything you've learned.

1293. When you don't know what to do, just remember that God does. Let Him prove it by you staying out of it.

SOMETHING ELSE CAN DO IT FOR YOU

1294. What you must do for yourself is to see that you cannot do it for yourself, after which it is done for you.

1295. It is a miracle moment when you perceive that change must come to you, you can't go to it.

1296. Right knowledge comes only from God. You will never get anything right from another human being.

1297. It is the absence of me that produces real change.

1298. When something that is not of your world begins to change your world, you will know it and know it surely and silently.

1299. If you want to know why things are the way they are, it is because things are the way they are. If you try to change the way things are, you will just keep them the way they are. Knowledge of this changes the way you are, which places you in a new and commanding relationship with the way things are.

BE IN CHARGE

1300. Suppose you are in a thick jungle with a cabin in the center. Your friends come and visit you. Among them are the hyena, the vulture, the little lamb and the crocodile. You begin to notice how these friends have taken over your home. They eat your food, watch your TV and come and go as they wish. You finally decide to take a stand. You go out to the porch where they are relaxing and tell them, "This is my home. This is my life. I am going to take charge of it from now on. Don't you dare come knocking on my door again and five minutes later try to con me.

You are either going to behave in a right relationship to me or you can just go back into that dark jungle and stay there.

"What I am trying to tell you is that from now on there is a new relationship between us in which I, a working human being not a fawning human being, am in charge of you and this jungle. And if you forget, I will remind you again. I will remind you until you hear and you may disappear."

Most of the animals will snarl and retreat into the jungle. They know that they cannot con you anymore and that the only place they can live is in the jungle. A few remain. They are the ones who want something different than being an animal. You find out there is no loneliness as long as you are what you're supposed to be, a self-complete human being not needing animals at all, because the animal part of you has gone.

1301. Sickos never know how patient ordinary people have to be with them. So when meeting anyone notice how you react to them, what's going through you when you talk to them. Let the little bit of virtue in you do the perceiving for you and you'll know exactly how to deal with them. Be glad when you see where this leads. For if you're fully in charge of yourself, living from the Spirit, that very high level immediately solves all problems you now have.

1302. Come on now, who knows more about running the universe, you or God?

1303. The life you can have is in charge of the entire universe.

INNER-WORK EXERCISES

THREE SECONDS It is right instruction to slow down and very beneficial to make small aims to do this. You will see how you forget to follow the simplest of instructions. This observation of failure is success. Make an aim to slow down your reaction for three seconds when someone speaks to you.

STUDY YOUR FEAR Practice this exercise intensely for one full week and be pleased and delighted by what you'll learn. You're to study your fear of somebody being angry or insolent toward you.

NO TO NEGATIVITY When you feel a negativity coming on or are in a negative state say, "No!" Get a right idea in your mind and do it. For example, "I am going to walk consciously" or "I am going to read a right book." Be aware of how you would rather go asleep. When you meet an inner or outer challenge, turn it towards staying awake. You have to work against yourself. You are the only enemy you have.

DOUBLE-DUTY Everyone you meet will try to get you to think for them, to make a decision. As an exercise, you will not only think for yourself but you will, as a conscious project, think for others. Be aware that they are shoving it onto you. Accept this work and watch your resentment. You are deliberately burdening yourself. Double your burden. Force your brain to wake up.

• • •

Chapter 7
TRUE WISDOM

THE SUPREME LAWS OF LIFE

1304. Only God is successful.

1305. God loves only what is like Himself.

1306. God can only allow His nature in Heaven. Only the kingdom of heaven on earth can inherit the Kingdom of Heaven.

1307. God is not a thought.

1308. God never punishes anyone. People punish themselves by preferring their own way.

1309. God will not compete with your sickness. God wants you 100% well and he will not settle for anything less.

1310. God is behind any and all efforts that a human being makes toward Him.

1311. God is here for a purpose. All you have to do is ask. Don't want to stay you. God will help you to choose something higher than yourself.

1312. When you go out, God comes in.

WHAT WE MUST SEE

1313. Both demons and angels have insight into human nature. Demons use it to destroy; angels use it to heal.

1314. The devil is very cunning but he's also very stupid.

1315. It is supremely good to see the bad.

1316. It is bad for you to be sick and neurotic and unhappy. Look at what you are trusting. See how dumb you really are. You are worshipping self-sickness, trusting it to lead you out. So suddenly examine your inner states from time to time, see how you operate wrongly and badly, and realize that remaining in self-punishment is bad for you. You are terrified right now that, if you were to understand this, something would be taken from you and you wouldn't know what to do. Exactly. Don't spend one more day going on as you are. Are you afraid you'll lose something good? What do you have that's good? Nothing. All you have is weakness, cowardice, a sheep-like mind. If Truth takes that away, you'll be able to walk free and live the life you want.

1317. Read the following phrase over a thousand times: Eternally connected to the supreme source.

1318. The test for receptivity is very simple: How many facts about myself will I hear that I don't want to hear?

1319. You don't have to be spiritually right. You need only see where you are mentally wrong.

1320. If I could stand on a mountaintop overlooking the entire world, I would shout down, "You don't know you're being taken."

1321. There was once a School of True Wisdom. An angel stood on guard before it, blocking entrance at the front gate. One morning a seeker approached the gate and asked admittance. The angel told him, "If I step aside and you enter here, you will see that you have been a shameless faker all your life." The seeker answered, "I wish to enter. Please step aside." The angel then said to the seeker, "If I step aside and you enter here, you must abandon all your usual and beloved hopes and ambitions." The seeker said, "I wish to come in.

Please step aside." The angel continued, "If I step aside and you enter here, you will come face to face with every evil and secret thought you have ever thought." The seeker replied, "I wish to go inside. Please step aside." The angel smiled and stepped aside.

ABOUT SIN AND FORGIVENESS

1322. The one time a sinner never sins is when he earnestly tries to understand his sinfulness.

1323. To refuse to develop is the greatest of all sins.

1324. Evil can be defined as non-evolvement, as not living up to possibilities of inner-development. Thus a tiger is not evil when he kills someone for he cannot evolve above his level of instinctive and mechanical behavior. But a man who kills another man is evil because he has failed to take his opportunity for rising above low-level instinctive and mechanical behavior.

1325. Sorry means you can't and won't do it again.

1326. Your repentance is false if you ask only for forgiveness. Your repentance is true only if you ask for both forgiveness and enlightenment.

1327. A refusal to understand my position in time is a refusal of my position in eternity.

1328. If you consciously know you've sinned, you'll be forgiven.

TRUE PRAYER

1329. It is vital that you bring sincere prayer back into your life. Say to God, "Dear God, I am the most afraid of losing myself. Please help me to use the power of choice the way you want me to."

155

1330. Your prayers, your requests, are what you are. For example, when you see that house you could have bought for $40,000 and it's now $140,000, you feel regret. The house is your crisis. You prayed for and got regret. There are hundreds of daily crises that arise. You think people have more money, have more friends, are younger, happier and healthier. Watch these thoughts over and over until you see what you are doing against yourself.

1331. How come your prayers aren't answered? In the first place, you want God—what you call God—to give you an advantage over someone else. Or you want God to unmake the mess you got into through your own ignorance and through your own vanity and through your own pride. And one of the worst things that can happen is to have an accidental answer that you attribute to God, because now you're even further into the illusion that, "If I pray in a certain way, God will answer this prayer."

1332. You have to send a prayer to Heaven and not to hell. Find out where you are praying to hell.

1333. The reason you have misery at 8 a.m. is because you prayed for it at 8 p.m.

1334. A right attitude is a right prayer.

1335. Have this marvelous attitude: May more of the Spirit of Truth course through me.

1336. God help me in spite of myself.

1337. God is always faithful and always answers true prayers.

1338. You need only one prayer to cover every difficulty in life. That prayer is, "I pray to see more."

1339. Morning prayer: "God help me to keep the integrity of my own mind all day."

INHERIT YOUR SPIRITUAL CASTLE

1340. Life must be built on spiritual plans.

1341. The spiritual castle begins to be built when you see that you can't do a thing from yourself to build it.

1342. Don't call your haunted house a castle.

1343. Evil has no permanent place to live. It only has shaky time structures in which to dwell. Evil is always roaming trying to find a place to settle down.

1344. By seeing what we fear to see, we shatter one of the pillars supporting the haunted house.

1345. The treasure is under the house, but you cannot find it without first tearing down the house.

1346. Don't be afraid to have nothing to do in your life. Don't fear to let your mind be emptied of what you now fill it with. Have no concern over not feeling the sour or explosive emotions that you now feel.

1347. Divine destruction is construction.

1348. The secret of spiritual success is to repeatedly let the house collapse on top of you so often and so watchfully that you finally see that there is neither a house to collapse nor anyone for it to collapse upon.

1349. Truth breaks you down so it can rebuild you according to its specifications in Heaven.

1350. The spiritual castle has no geographical location on this earth. It does not exist in the woods or outside the woods. It exists above both, in a new and lofty world.

THE KINGDOM OF HEAVEN

1351. The Kingdom of Heaven is located in the space between two thoughts. Enter that space and you enter the Kingdom of Heaven. You must make a connection between the "bang-bang" succession of thoughts and the fact that you are always nervous. Become completely unconnected with what you see.

1352. You must get above the mind to enter into the Kingdom of Heaven—*above the mind.*

1353. The Kingdom of Heaven is pure intelligence.

1354. One department in Heaven consists of never having to tell yourself and convince yourself that you are right and others are wrong.

1355. Dedicate yourself more and more each day to God and His Kingdom. Entering the Kingdom, *entering it,* is the only important thing on this earth.

1356. To most human beings, the Kingdom of Heaven is the kingdom of self.

1357. Only the willing go to Heaven.

1358. The Kingdom of Heaven never suffers and neither will you when you are there.

THE ONLY POWER YOU NEED

1359. When you have God in your life, what else do you need?

1360. To enter the Kingdom of Heaven you must give up all wishes for power.

1361. Arguing over anything including spiritual things is always wrong. An arguer tries to make his personal belief look like a universal truth, which is both impossible and frustrating.

1362. He who argues does not know. His argument is a useless attempt to fight off the horde of doubts charging out from his own false position. Hostile argument can use words, cold eyes, abrupt physical movements, even a defensive tilt of the head. But of course the arguer, who has never studied himself, is foolishly unaware of how he gives himself away.

1363. When someone screams out to affirm his position, it is not the position which he values, but the screaming itself. He screams to try to convince himself that he has a position that is real and beneficial. His actual position is in the center of delusion. He is a prisoner in the castle dungeon, hallucinating that his position is on the castle throne.

1364. A naturally quiet mind is the only power you need. Truth is quiet. It has no need to prove itself at all.

1365. Want no power except from God.

HOW TO LEARN ABOUT GOD

1366. You learn about God by learning about Satan. You learn about Satan by learning about God.

1367. Satan is single-minded. Truth is single-spirited.

1368. Spirit must be the master, with thought an obedient servant. For most men thought is the master and spirit is a hated enemy.

1369. The intellect is an atheist incapable of understanding anything above itself. The intellect can never know God. It can only create false gods including mechanical religion, hero-worship, greed for money or power.

159

1370. The condemnation you feel for being evil comes only from evil itself, never from God. The condemnation is nothing more than the unnatural storm arising from your present confused nature. This means that the curse on you comes from you.

1371. I will explain to you why you're not happy, why you're not carefree. It's because you're trying to collect things. You're a collector, and you think that every time you get one of those objects that you desire so fervently it adds something to you, to your security. Well, I would guess that if you take paper and pencil and write down all the things you've acquired—friends, romances, exciting occasions, physical objects—it would number in the thousands, wouldn't it, tens of thousands of things that you have possessed for a few seconds or maybe several years? Maybe you've had that house for fifty years for example. How come you're still worried?

1372. You have never trusted God to prove to you that He has a supreme gift for you, which is a life that is different from the one you now falsely treasure.

1373. If you know unlife when you see it, you will know Life when you see it.

1374. At the split second that you know of the existence of Satan, you will also know of the existence of God.

KNOWING AND WHOLENESS

1375. Something exists that you do not see. Right now everything is done. It's complete. Accept!

1376. Understand that you are only a receiver of what has already been created.

1377. If you want to know who you are not, you are not your biography of yourself.

1378. I will know who I am when memory no longer describes me.

1379. I know who I really am when I don't think about who I am.

1380. There is *knowing* but there is no *knower.*

1381. There is really no individual person who sees or understands anything. There is only pure and impersonal seeing and understanding. This becomes clear when you are able to talk about yourself without believing in the self you talk about, which is the same as conscious talking.

1382. Knowing is the absence of ignorance.

1383. "I" can't know God. The "un-I" can know God.

1384. When in a state of *I don't know,* there is a knowing which is total and universal and not a personal possession.

1385. I just want you to know how well I know you. You have a mind screaming with nightmares. Be honest enough to admit you have just heard an accurate description—you have a mind screaming with nightmares. By the way, the solution is also known if you want to know it. All you know are your ideas about God, the catch phrases, a few words, but you don't know God at all. Therefore you don't know how to make proper contact in order to get help—help being the dissolution of you. That is the help you are given in this class.

1386. Wholeness does not reside in thinking about wholeness but in the lack of a need to think about wholeness.

1387. Self-wholeness is self-niceness.

WISDOM IS BEYOND WORDS

1388. A truly spiritual teacher finds it easier to see a high truth than to explain it to lower minds. This is because the explanatory words used by the teacher have multiple meanings to the pupil based on the pupil's associations and preferences connected with the words. For example, the word "progress" could be unknowingly interpreted by the pupil as meaning progress in being praised for steady attendance in class. The explanation of all this by the teacher to the student will also be distorted by the student. If the teacher uses the word "association," the pupil's mind could actually send up a picture of a business association. This is the interference of a human idea that prevents divine perception.

1389. We read a truth, a fact. And then we very easily get careless with it, forget it or think we already understand it. So do bring yourself back to simply thinking about and reflecting on, a fundamental truth—and you can't get one that is too simple. Don't make the mistake, which so many people make who come to these classes for the first time, of thinking you already understand something simply because you understand the words. There is a great difference between familiarity with a word, perhaps the word "love," and understanding and actually living the state which this word represents.

1390. When using a truthful idea, you must realize that it is simply an idea to eventually rise above. A mental picture of a glass of water cannot satisfy thirst. Only actual water can satisfy. The idea of water comes first but then you must go beyond it to secure actual water. Lost human beings take the idea of water as water itself.

1391. Are you listening to the meaning behind the speaker's words or are you reacting to your own negative interpretation of his words?

1392. Detect the point at which your ordinary mind cannot follow a truth.

1393. You don't have to change yourself. There is no way you can change yourself. You need only realize that you have no separate self to change. You need only transcend your belief in a personal self. Having done this, say that you can't change yourself, and a minute later you can say that you can change yourself. These statements by the use of opposite language will contain no contradiction. An awakened mind can use opposing statements without getting caught between them. Such a mind is like an explorer on a high hill, safely watching two fighting lions below him.

1394. Don't try to do with the mind what can only be done with the Spirit.

1395. You have to take these truths and let it be received by the Spirit of Truth in you rightly so it is not distorted by your mind.

1396. You have risen above mere words when you see no difference between the phrases of self-reliance and heavenly reliance.

SPIRITUAL TRANSFORMATION

1397. Whoever I think I am changes at every new second. Therefore, memory cannot establish a permanent self which can do something the next minute or year.

1398. Human interest in studying human evil produces the miracle of self-transformation.

1399. When watching a movie, be sure to remain in the audience and not join the action on the screen.

1400. I falsely love what I see because I falsely love what I am. I see only what I am. I am only what I see. When seen through, the net of ideas stops and inner division stops.

1401. Here is a curious contradiction of the ordinary mind. A man wants others to think well of him, yet believes himself to be the lowest of the low. This is a perfect example of the alternating roles of the false self. It will play the part of either a good or a bad person, just as long as the actor can think about its own make-believe existence.

1402. A simple switch in your viewpoint will swiftly increase your insight into yourself and others. Here is the switch: See another person as a mass of inner conditions, not a unified outer personality. This detaches your own distorting likes and dislikes toward someone, freeing the clear vision of nondesire.

1403. Now I am serious, you listen to me. When you're able to say very quietly and calmly, "How stupid I have been!" When that revelation comes to you, you then have one foot in Heaven. Now you're beginning to know what self-abandonment means. And the greatest joy of your day will be finding at least one more way to get rid of that sick impostor you thought was you. What a pleasure to get rid of one a day.

1404. Spiritual Transformation is really a lessening of the inner population.

PROTECT THE CANDLELIGHT

1405. Every human being is possessed either by Light or darkness.

1406. Anyone weary of stumbling in the dark has taken the first step toward walking in the Light.

1407. One little candlelight of sincerity can meet any situation.

1408. We learn to love the Light by seeing clearly what the darkness does to us.

1409. Some people are more weak than evil. Some people are more evil than weak. The one who is more weak than evil has a chance. The one who is more evil than weak does not have a chance.

1410. Those who are wasting their lives are not merely willing but are quite eager for you to waste your own life. This statement has no meaning at all to those who will continue to waste their own lives.

1411. Realize that there is only one thing you can trust, which is the Light itself.

1412. No one can fall under the evil influence of another unless he is already under the evil influence of himself.

1413. All marauding thoughts and moods must be brought from the unconscious up to the conscious, so that Spiritual Light can take them away.

1414. Above all else in your life, protect the candle-light.

HELL

1415. Hell consists of sensing that you cannot turn your lie into the truth.

1416. Hell consists of being a wrong person who angrily and hatefully tries to prove that he is a right person. This will become clearer as you imagine a man frantically trying to prove to others that nighttime is daytime.

1417. The purpose of Satan is to kill and destroy.

1418. Evil has one aim, to drag you down to the level of hell that it is on.

1419. The devil is unconsciousness.

1420. The first rule of hell is: *Drag as many in as you can.*

1421. Never mind a future hell, pay attention to this one.

1422. Hell is talking to yourself for no reason.

1423. If you were ready I could take you by the hand and take you on a trip through hell. I could show you not only the secret rooms but the secret rooms within the secret rooms.

1424. The deeper you go into your own hell, the higher you will go into Heaven.

1425. If you visit hell willingly there is no way it can endure.

1426. Never mind what you have to go through to get this. Give up everything. Then you won't live in hell anymore.

ANGER IS ALWAYS HARMFUL

1427. Are you aware that you must personally live with your own burning and tormenting hatred?

1428. When you are angry, you are not happy.

1429. People like to claim they have no hatred in them, which means a main hate is to see and admit their hatred.

1430. Concealed anger is the cunning killer.

1431. Anger to others is mocking God.

1432. The burning feeling of hatred is the hater's idea of happiness.

1433. All hostility is enmity against God.

1434. This sentence is worth a week of pondering: I am angry with myself because I believe in myself the wrong way.

1435. The next time I am angry at a person or a condition, I will comment to myself as follows: "Maybe I am really angry at my own weakness and inability to handle the condition."

1436. When you are rageful at getting pushed around, try to see you are getting pushed around only by your rage at getting pushed around.

1437. Don't you ever accept anger in yourself or others as being right. If you will refuse to accept anger, hostility and hatred—this inner violence—as right and necessary, you will then begin to see where the actual cause of your problems is. You now justify violence in yourself and others you are allied with. They hate the same things you do and you justify each other's hatred.

1438. Hostility is an enemy of God and goodness.

1439. Yes, you can pretend that you don't have hostility, and you can also disguise it by calling it by another name, but in either case you will be punished by your hostility. Why not invite Truth to dissolve both the hostility and its punishment?

1440. Little by little, step by step, see what happens to you as you deliberately abandon your rage and hostility.

HOW TO DEFEAT THE DEVIL

1441. Listen carefully when the devil whispers and in his stupidity he will show you exactly how to defeat him. For example, he will tell you that winning an advantage over others is all that makes life worth living. Study that shallow propaganda and then tell the devil something. Tell him that you have won a thousand times like that and still have not won.

1442. You must absolutely destroy what is absolutely trying to destroy you.

1443. Every time you break down, which is whenever you get negative, remember that you must never enter the lunatic asylum to try to straighten out the inmates. They will only combine to attack you.

1444. Don't throw rocks at Satan. That's what he wants.

1445. I don't have to answer an angry world.

1446. The struggle comes to an end when there is no *for* and *against*.

1447. The awareness of insanity can't be part of it.

1448. Think right now of the worst thing you ever did. You are not that. Evil forces took you over and made you do that horrible thing twenty years ago. Purification of memory can free you right now of that wrong thing you did twenty years or twenty minutes ago.

1449. Since imagination has taken the place of reality, you must first destroy imagination in your life by listening to yourself, watching yourself behave, actually catching yourself in your secret thoughts with your hidden motives. This is so you can in time learn what is good for you, so you can choose the right over what is habitual and easy and popular. All that has to be broken down by something you have invited in, by consciousness. To get your reward, you must do your work. You must follow the exercises!

1450. The devil is already defeated.

1451. With long hard work, some day the dark forces will have no choice but to leave you.

1452. Let it be a rightly comforting thought that God knows everything about you.

UNDERSTAND EVIL

1453. Evil can be described as ignorance of the need to develop inwardly.

1454. The purpose of evil is to prevent you from entering the Kingdom of Heaven.

1455. Evil is nothing more than being in a state of unconsciousness, of being asleep.

1456. There is a certain horrible pleasure in being asleep.

1457. Someone makes a gloomy remark and you think you have to take it and react to it. The only reason they give you the poison is because you accept it. They have no choice but to want you to be as they are. They know all the gimmicks and tricks to keep you reaching out and accepting it. When conversing with others, I want you to know what that other person said to you. I want you to notice his spirit and see if he makes some small negative remark. See if the negativity consists of a certain facial expression, a certain manner, even the way he carries himself. When you see how your weariness and discouragement are caused by accepting the poison, this will give you the strength to refuse it.

1458. A human being who loves the dark must add more and more weight to himself to continue to feel the pain and torture he loves.

1459. The devil's aim with you and everyone else is to torment you at your weakest point. That is where he will attempt to discourage you.

1460. The devil will use every trick he can to stop you.

1461. Nothing is too low for a devil to do.

1462. An evil man slanders the Truth because of the hell he feels for doing it.

1463. Delirious drifters are deceitful and dangerous.

1464. The dark forces are parasites and can't exist without your cooperation.

1465. You don't know how alert you have to be to refuse the flood of insanity!

1466. All conflict is between two opposing evil counterparts. There is no fight, no struggle at all between Light and darkness.

WHAT SATAN CAN'T STAND

1467. Dark forces have one fatal flaw: You can find out about them.

1468. When the darkness is brought up to Light, the Light destroys the darkness all by itself without your help. Light is fatal to darkness.

1469. Evil has no right to exist.

1470. The very act of catching evil as it starts to form stops it.

1471. Dark forces can dish it out but they can't take it. They are weak and cowardly and they run away in the presence of Truth and insight.

1472. Throughout all the history of eternity, no devil has ever tricked his way into the Kingdom of God.

1473. You have the power to smash entirely the false power of evil that has dominated your life.

1474. Armed with this heavenly power, you will have one dominating reply to the devil, which is, "Get along your way." When you firmly tell the devil, "Get along your way," you smashingly defeat his cunning purpose of making you believe that you have something in common with him.

1475. Truth is the strongest sword in the universe.

1476. Never forget the next forceful fact: When you reply to the devil from the Spirit of Heaven, the devil must obey your command. He has no choice but to obey. The devil is helpless in the face of true spiritual authority, just as darkness must slink away with the bright light of the rising sun.

1477. The demons live in disgust and hatred toward that one man or woman that passes beyond the line where the demons cannot live.

BREAKING THE CHAINS OF SUFFERING

1478. Everything you need to know for self-rescue can be known. Anything you can't know is not necessary for you to know. Self-rescue is all that matters. All knowledge for attaining it is open to your receptivity.

1479. The self you suffer over does not exist. But this is something we all must work hard to understand for ourselves.

1480. In the spiritual life, only self-failure succeeds.

1481. To advance, you need authentically new experiences. One of them is to remain with the pain. Now you want to get rid of the pain and replace it with excitement, comfort, etc.

1482. Do you want a guaranteed spiritual formula for becoming mentally and spiritually healthy? Try to have as many devastating experiences as possible consciously. Oh, you have them now but you don't take them rightly. You hate them or use them as an excuse to go blab to your friends about how badly life has treated such a precious person as you. You enjoy your pain. That becomes a new possession. If you're smart, when you ask God to destroy your present ridiculous strutting little life, you will add a second prayer and ask God to enable you to meet experiences properly, with a wise spiritual mind instead of with your usual egotism. One collapse is fine. Two collapses are good. Three are great. Four are terrific. Five are stupendous.

1483. Try to do something in the next twenty-four hours that will make your vanity scream and protest.

1484. Spiritual heroism is when you do what is right even while feeling threatened by something inside you which opposes what is right.

1485. There is a way to break the chains of fear and suffering. Place the thought-self in a dangerous and scary position and keep it there.

ASK HEAVEN FOR HELP

1486. May I please have more Light?

1487. Affection for the Truth is always rewarded.

1488. God, I want to love you but I can't. Please help me.

1489. Truth wants only to help you. Falsehood wants only to hurt you.

1490. Truth can cleanse you if you yield.

1491. You must love Truth more than you love your life.

1492. God is your toughness. Don't you try to do it on your own.

1493. Say, "Please Heaven, fight for me, for I can't fight for myself."

1494. Let the Light fight and all will be right.

1495. There is nothing too much for who you really are.

WHAT WE NEED

1496. We need all the help we can get.

1497. If you can take it, you will make it.

1498. How ruthless can you be with yourself? How can you refuse the little catnaps that the devil has prepared for you? Take defending yourself. Even if the accusation is true, why are we so quick to explain, "Here's why I did that." Why don't you be quiet so you can see this false part of you wanting to defend yourself and give no explanation at all? You are tied to people with your own defenses.

1499. Only a personal internal earthquake is going to wake you up.

1500. There is a source of healing higher than your mind. Try to bear it. Try to endure being healed.

1501. Make everything, every day, as hard as possible on yourself. Be awake to the environment without thinking about it with this objective: to go through a new hell, a healing hell of not knowing what to do. Hell is the avoidance of hell. Go right up to it and go through it. You cannot lift the curse of ignorance on yourself unless you are willing to let the hell blaze as furiously as it wishes—and it wishes to blaze far more furiously than you have ever dared to see, which is why you're suppressed and cursed. Do you really care more for the inner dictator than for your deliverance? Go through the hell of a supposed *you* disappearing.

1502. You have one thing and one thing only to give to Truth. It is called obedience.

1503. Obedience to Truth gives Life.

1504. You have tried everything to solve your problems and nothing has worked out? May I suggest a radical solution? Try being normal.

1505. You are going to have to practice conscious defiance. This means to deliberately walk right down in the middle of hell because you understand at last that you are already in hell. You have to be willing to give up everything for the answer and you don't even know if there is an answer. The initiative has to be yours to descend down where it gets hotter and hotter and hotter. You have to be willing to be all alone down there— no friends, no relatives, no hope. The answer is for you to endure unto the end. And gradually your little petty jealousies and your dependency on others are consumed.

1506. It is good, right and necessary that Truth should overwhelm you.

UNDERSTANDING TIME AND DEATH

1507. It is my duty to show you the difference between death and Life, so you can make the choice.

1508. Your true self was never born so it can never die.

1509. Ignorance is not knowing that ignorance is temporary.

1510. Death is when there is opposition to growth.

1511. Never forget this key point: You don't let go because you fear the death of your false life.

1512. The death of mechanical thought is the death of *me*, therefore, the death of misery and the birth of eternity. Thoughts do not enter Heaven.

1513. You can escape time. Then when you die, the death of the body will mean absolutely nothing to you.

1514. Your honest admission that you're living in death will open the door to Life.

1515. The time-self does not have everlasting Life; the timeless-self does.

1516. The *me* is nothing but impulses, opinions, ideas. If you can see that the *me* consists of that and that is the problem, the problem-creator in the first place, then the whole question of death—"What is going to happen to me after death?"—disappears. Who is the *me*? If you could die to the *me* now so that it does not exist now, would the question come up? Or does the false me create the question? If there is no *me*, is the question still valid?

1517. Time is always pain because it's separated from God.

1518. The purpose of life is easily explained. We aim to die before we die physically, in order to live before we die in order to live beyond death.

1519. When you really know you have no life to lose, you will finally have a life you can't lose.

TIME AND ETERNITY

1520. Love eternity, not this life.

1521. This is a moment in eternity.

1522. Most people want to pretend they are going to live forever.

1523. The physical cannot follow you into eternity.

1524. A deluded mind takes the repetition of time-events as the eternal state.

1525. You can never prove that an illusion is the truth.

1526. Proving your nonexistence in time is the same as proving your existence in eternity.

1527. Eternity can understand time, but time cannot understand eternity.

1528. Time as measured by the calendar has nothing whatsoever to give you.

1529. You inherit eternity by dissolving time while still in it.

1530. You want to think your way into eternity and it can't be done.

1531. The reason you cannot think about eternity is because the intellect which is doing the thinking is an instrument of time and nothing else.

1532. Anything that lives in time must topple.

1533. Time can neither understand nor enter eternity. Only eternity understands eternity.

1534. Time is my thoughts, my physical body, my attitudes. They are not part of my real nature. Neither are my past and future. When I understand that, then the sensing of nowness, which is eternity, takes its place. Nowness then directs the present time-nature intelligently without conceit or self-centeredness.

1535. When you decide to become nothing in your own eyes and nothing in the eyes of other people, that nothingness is eternal life.

1536. When you really understand that the Truth lives forever so will you.

1537. Why do you anxiously yearn for eternal life? It is because it represents another kind of existence which you think is superior to your present troubled life. You want something different, which you call everlasting life. If you will simply be happy in your present life, which can be done, you will never again anxiously yearn for eternal life but will have it. Your present spiritual health and intelligence is eternal life.

1538. Let the perishable perish. Let the immortal be immortal. There it is, the entire secret.

TRUE SALVATION

1539. Think about the miracle of saving yourself.

1540. God is watching you to see when you will give up *your* plan of salvation and accept *His*.

1541. You need never seek salvation. You need only know that you don't have it.

1542. True spiritual salvation begins when you see that you are a part of the mad mob and that the last thing you want is to be rescued. You must see how violently you fight your own salvation.

1543. Against your own wishes, you have to let God save you.

1544. Don't believe in instant salvation. All of that is a cruel hoax. There is no such thing. It comes gradually, over years and years of hard persistent work.

1545. You are saved by seeing sin in the present and not pleasures in the future.

1546. Think of this key idea: When you have no future you are saved.

1547. First I am one with my sickness. Then I stand apart and see my sickness. Then I am one with my wholeness.

1548. When you no longer try to save yourself, God can save you and He will.

CHRIST

1549. Christ taught that you don't have to be you anymore.

1550. The purpose of your life is for you personally to be resurrected, to find out what Christ did, what the purpose of His lesson was.

1551. What can be more important than for your name to be written in the Book of Life?

1552. Christ used His physical body to teach a spiritual point.

1553. The resurrection lesson that Christ taught is all about you being different. When Christ rose on the third day, He no longer lived in the world of this physical earth, of Galilee, of Jerusalem, of the Mount of Olives, of disciples, of enemies or Pharisees and scribes.

When He rose, He rose to a new way, a new life, a spiritual life, and this is what He tried to illustrate with His own life. To be resurrected, to be born again, means to not care for anything that belongs to this world, including the physical body, including the way your mind works now, including your desires and recreations, your plans and pursuits.

To be resurrected means to be resurrected *ABOVE* the earth, above yourself, above enemies, above petty little pleasures. It means being resurrected above every single item that has to do with darkness, tension, thinking uselessly, rambling around inside your mind wildly. To be a new man, a new woman means just that. And one way to describe it means that you no longer care what you are required to lose because you understand that loss must precede gain.

1554. You have to die to everything that is wrong about you.

1555. Do you think the King of the universe would visit your mind the way it is now?

1556. The resurrection can occur in this life, in this physical body. It's an inward thing, an invisible thing. It is not something you do, it is something that happens to you.

1557. Rising above yourself, in case you didn't know it, simply means to rise above nothing.

1558. Obedience to the Truth is the how.

1559. When you are willing to die and fall down on the ground psychologically, Truth will be able to come and talk with you because now you will listen where you would never listen before.

1560. Resurrection happens when you are no longer trying to make things happen.

1561. As the Bible says, "Ponder these things in your heart."

1562. Christ said, "Those things I have done, ye can do also."

ALL IS WELL

1563. Just as there are millions of unseen stars, there are endless inner riches for you to discover.

1564. It is better to be healthy than to be sick.

1565. God is sending truth-waves at all times.

1566. Truth alone is now my source of instruction. So all is well. I rest. All is well, now and forever.

1567. At last all is well. How do I know? Because I know that at last I am well.

INNER-WORK EXERCISES

LOOK ABOVE When you meet any human being, no matter where you go or whoever he is, when you first meet him look a yard above him. Let this remind you that there is God, who is above all human beings.

SELF-SURPRISING   To produce the necessary jolt to see that you don't know where you are, learn self-surprising. Pull a trick on the devil. Do this exercise by yourself or with someone else. When tempted to react with a harsh word or hostile feeling, just endure the uncertainty of not knowing what will happen. Then you will understand what has enslaved you all these years.

DARING THE DEVIL   When you fall apart before other people and they see through your fakery, you must make immediate correction. You must immediately walk into a second scary situation where you will again fall apart, preferably with double the disgrace than before. This technique is known as daring the devil to do his worst. The poor devil will do his best to do his worst, which will be a revealing act to witness. When you see who really possesses the disgrace, you will also see the devil flee in disgrace.

FACE THE ENEMY   When you finally face the enemy, every attacker will go away. Eventually something happens to you that is not from you. Exorcise yourself with an exercise: Go home, get paper, write *Exorcise with Exercises* on the top and then, in separate short numbered items, write everything you know that exposes foreign, evil forces for what they are—fakes! Keep them short little items. And go over the list every day, even when you don't want to. Dark forces are fakes.

• • •

Chapter 8
THE SPIRITUAL IS PRACTICAL

BE NEW EVERY MOMENT

1568. Doesn't the sameness continue from day to day?

1569. Several goldfish were swimming inside their glass bowl. Complained one of them, "Around and around we go, tired and bored, never seeing anything new." Agreed another goldfish, "Yes, you would think the Great Starfish in his supreme wisdom would have created a world larger than a goldfish bowl."

1570. Boredom is time.

1571. Your god is what you think about all day long.

1572. The false self can only repeat itself.

1573. Darkness tells you a great big lie. Darkness tells you the new can come out of the old.

1574. Stop calling on troubles to end troubles. Stop calling on the old nature to dissolve the old nature. Stop calling the enemy soldier your friend.

1575. Get off the treadmill. You think the illusion of constant motion is taking you somewhere. It isn't!

1576. Be new every moment.

1577. The Path is the only thing that will not bore.

GIVE NO THOUGHT FOR TOMORROW

1578. You need not give a single thought to what happened to you in past years nor a single thought to future years. You need only know what you are doing right now.

1579. The nature of the will of God is easily explained. It is simply what is really good for you regardless of how you presently think otherwise. Deep insight into this takes the pain out of unexpected events and replaces it with an ease that you don't think about.

1580. If you look forward to being happy, you will never be happy.

1581. True Life is never a repeat performance. Life is something that has no relationship to what went before.

1582. Let your aim be to move closer to God with each passing second.

1583. The present moment is the enemy of lost people.

1584. No one is asked to give up enjoyment. He is asked to abandon his false concept of enjoyment so that true refreshment may enter every moment.

1585. You need not add to your already complete true self and you cannot add to a nonexistent false self. Relax.

1586. Fifty years of internal damage done by the time-self is healed instantaneously by the entrance of the eternal self.

THE POWER OF INSTANT RECOVERY

1587. Each time I become aware of myself, I start life all over.

1588. Whenever you are disturbed by something, upset or nervous, you've been carried away. I want you to know that you can recover instantly and come back to solid ground.

1589. You ladies are instructed not to break down and

giggle foolishly when in a crisis, like spilling the coffee, for example. You are to remain poised. You know it happened, but you need not let anyone looking at you, nor their attitude toward you, nor anything inside you take away your poise. Walk through this world and don't look left or right. I don't care what it is, you walk forward and no one will be able to stop you. Remember the lesson, *Instant Recovery.* Don't you dare let anyone intimidate you.

1590. Instant observation of your weakness when it expresses itself is absolutely essential.

1591. Yesterday's wild thoughts have no power to intrude into today's mind.

1592. Instant recovery cancels time.

1593. When you know there is no self to start life all over, life starts all over.

1594. You are new right now.

THE PAST IS THE PAST

1595. God is not concerned about your past, you are!

1596. The past contaminates the present.

1597. You don't have a past; you just think you do.

1598. Anything left in time will fade of itself.

1599. The present moment is entirely free.

NOW IS NEW

1600. Heaven is to not live in time.

1601. Cancel time and space and stay where you are right now.

1602. If you're willing enough, God will be right there.

1603. When you really know where you are, there is nothing to do but calmly be where you are.

1604. Right thought is thinking about the right thing at the right time. What you should be thinking about is what you are doing right now.

1605. Hope is hopeless because you're always pushing away the present moment.

1606. The devil's pitchfork is in time.

1607. The now is always safe.

1608. Always stay where you are. The solution will come to you and you will fly freely.

1609. You must give up all, everything, without knowing what you will have next.

1610. There is no next. There is only a series of nows.

1611. Now is new because it doesn't include you.

SOLVE THE MYSTERY OF WHO

1612. Who am I talking about? Who am I thinking about? Who am I feeling about?

1613. What will you sacrifice to be who you really are?

1614. There is no self to glorify. How can you glorify yourself when there's no self to start with? You can't put a crown on a nonexistent person. You can't put jewels on him. You can't give him money because there's no one there, there's nothing there. It's all a mirage, all a delusion, all madness. Your observation of your madness will lead to sanity.

1615. It seems like a hopeless situation. But who is it hopeless for?

185

1616. There is no one there to let go of anyone. Your realization that there's no one there to let go is what letting go is.

1617. The purpose of life is to find out what is real. The purpose of life is to free yourself. The purpose of life is to understand all these false desires and wishes to protect, to cling to what you call your life. To find out the purpose of life requires a certain kind of responsibility on your part and that responsibility is to do more than other people, to stay all alone. Others, unless surrounded by like-minded people, unless they are flattered, don't know who they are. How long will you endure not going along with the crowd and say, "This is not for me."

YOU MUST MAKE CONNECTIONS

1618. A person who suffers from a loss or heartache or crisis cannot understand why it happened to him. This is very characteristic of a foggy mind. It cannot look back and see the firm connection between his careless cause and its shocking effect.

1619. One way in which we can create understanding is to make connections between ideas. Here are examples of how two ideas that don't seem to go together can be put together. Your part is to see how all ideas are connected to each other. Connect *demands* with *a dull life*, *dizzy thinking* with *cunning*, *false values* with *confusion*.

1620. Do you know that you have a deep fear of being patient? You fear patience. You say, "I've got to make a choice." Patience is the absence of you. Patience is the absence of self.

1621. Learning from experience consists of remembering

all that happened in a past event when meeting a new event.

1622. Connect the way you feel, your heaviness, with the fact of your unexposed weakness and evil.

1623. Are you gloomy? If you are, you have a peculiar love-hate relationship with yourself and everyone you meet.

1624. If you bound others, you bound yourself. If you free others, you free yourself.

1625. The more Truth you get the more you want.

1626. The lessons will come so fast that there is no way you can write them down. But don't worry. They are there and you can never lose them.

TAKE RIGHT INITIATIVE

1627. "Teacher, help me by making my daily decisions for me."

"Student, I will help you even more than that. I free you to develop inwardly by letting you make your own daily decisions."

1628. If we waited for the perfect student, we'd never have a class.

1629. For heaven's sake, grow up. You have to do the work yourself. There is no big daddy to do the work for you.

1630. If you have no spiritual initiative of your own, you will unknowingly try to steal initiative from those who have it. But you will go nowhere and you will feel your emptiness.

1631. I want to tell all of you in this room, yes all of you, you haven't begun to work on yourself in near the capacity that you could.

187

1632. A passive state of learning will never make it in the spiritual world.

1633. You have the knowledge. Now do what you know.

1634. Asking a question of another is easy, which doesn't mean you don't ask questions. Do the hard thing with yourself. Answer your own questions. Otherwise, they will remain unsolved.

STAY WITH THE PAIN

1635. An outlaw to Truth is an in-law to pain.

1636. To the degree that you are in pain you are wrong.

1637. All solutions proposed by pain only keep it going.

1638. The reason I can't do anything about my pain is because the only self I have at the moment of pain is the pain itself. When clearly understanding this, I stop trying to end the pain and that conscious act is precisely what ends the pain.

1639. If you forget your shocking pain, you will have to repeat it. Remember it. Let's say something "good" happens in the exterior world. For example, you get a raise. You then forget the pain you had before you got the raise, so are right back where you started. The next time you feel psychological pain, you will stay with it. If you stick with it, it will go away of itself, which is not a distraction. You are going to remember it as long as you can. If it comes back, you are going to stay with it and remember it.

1640. Humiliation is a valuable shaking of my flattering self-picture. Let it shake.

1641. Submitting to humiliation and admitting I was wrong is the healthy act of voluntarily entering my own unconscious hell.

1642. What's wrong with knowing you're a total disgrace? The more disgrace the better.

1643. The gold comes at the highest point of humiliation, at the moment of your worst tears and shames.

1644. What is unfortunate for your so-called dignity is fortunate for you.

1645. Disgrace is painful only to the disgraceful parts in us.

1646. Bear the pain of letting your pain go.

1647. There is no doubt about it, an avoided pain must be suffered again and again. When avoidance is ended, the pain is ended.

1648. Since I must have no god but God, I will stop worshipping my pain.

RIGHT AND LIGHT SERIOUSNESS

1649. Smile! Nothing bad will happen to you.

1650. Don't confuse unconscious gloom with seriousness.

1651. Heaviness often poses as seriousness. So sudden laughter in class has value, as a log tossed in front of the runaway truck which believes it is sincerely speeding toward a planned destination.

1652. Let cheerfulness circulate inside of you.

1653. You tell me that there is no reason for a sense of humor, that you have nothing to make you laugh. I tell you that you do, which is your own ridiculous daily attempts to win approval. This absurd drama can at least make you alternate between laughs and tears.

1654. Real seriousness is very light and very powerful and very effective.

1655. When feeling delirious, just go serious. Suddenly come back to yourself and notice the state you are presently in and go serious, which means you recognize you were in a wrong state.

1656. Right seriousness is right happiness.

A SACRED PLACE

1657. Any goodness that any human being has ever had did not come from his own mental movements. It is something that entered him from above but not something that he created.

1658. Think from above this world.

1659. The lower must never be allowed to interfere with the higher.

1660. Dark and low parts of you want to keep you a regular customer.

1661. Evil is subtle and gradual in taking over.

1662. The devil is a creeper.

1663. Every evil act is a representation of the entire kingdom of evil. The entire kingdom of evil operates through billions of little evils.

1664. Dirty jokes violate the sanctity of your inner life.

1665. Your mind is a sacred place. Now what is the right attitude toward a sacred place?

1666. You really do have to remember God. The world has forgotten God.

KNOW FROM YOURSELF

1667. You need not accept the existence of anything until it exists for you personally.

1668. Any man who tells you to reject present self-investigation in favor of a future spiritual or political heaven is living in his present hell. If you don't believe this, tell this fact to such a man. Watch him break down into confusion and anger, which is his present hell.

1669. The reason you should get understanding is because it will prevent misunderstanding.

1670. Unconcious desperation knows only what it wants and never anything else, such as decent public behavior.

1671. Badness is an admission of failure. Think about this all day.

YIELD TO TRUTH

1672. Make room for Truth.

1673. Truth never chases anyone. Its procedure is to match the retreat or the advance of the individual. Take one step away from Truth and it will take one step away from you. Take one step toward Truth and it will take one step toward you.

1674. If you don't yield you will break. If you yield you will not break.

1675. Be a conscious doormat.

1676. Don't waste your life.

1677. There is something you can have that will fight for you.

1678. We are simply wasting our lives unless we yield to Truth.

WELCOME HIGHER FACTS

1679. If you make an effort to act right, you will act wrong.

1680. My thoughts are not my thoughts.

1681. Know that distress and disappointment are states of stupidity and nothing else. Do not trust them. They have no intelligence whatever in them; they can only lead you astray. You are very foolish in being lured after their frantic shrieks. They shout that they are right, but they are always wrong, and wrong for you personally.

1682. You get more out of a *No* from life than you do from a *Yes*.

1683. The chief crime you are committing against yourself is that you refuse to become wise.

1684. There are definitely such things as evil spirits who roam the earth with malicious intentions. Having no life of their own, they seek to invade and inhabit individual humans. Remember this point: Since evil spirits have no life of their own they are insanely compelled to try to take over human bodies, which they succeed in doing. This is what is commonly called demon-possession. However, few demon-possessed individuals reveal their condition with abnormal public behavior. The fact is that most demon-possessed people appear to be quite normal, even noble, and many occupy powerful positions in society's affairs.

1685. No matter how much you give to a sick mind it is never enough. Don't be so stupid as to think that a hyena will thank you for giving him one ounce of meat. The big blunder is to give him anything in the first place.

1686. You are trying to reach the place where you can say, "No one can hurt me now." Trying to reach it prevents you from reaching it.

1687. Only eternity can keep you safe.

1688. Welcome higher facts without understanding them and in time you will understand.

FREEDOM FROM FUTURE EXPECTATIONS

1689. If life won't let you succeed, who said you had to?

1690. Hope for the future wrecks the future.

1691. We can no more enjoy life by hoping for a future result than we can enjoy music by waiting for the final note.

1692. All expectations are self-destructive because they are in time.

1693. You are tied down to your future with a rope of thoughts.

1694. No one is nice unless he can be so without nice possessions and nice advantages. May heaven help you if you cling to your supposed advantages, your securities, your comforts. Anything you look forward to will destroy you as it already has.

1695. Try to sense that there is a truly unique reward, but do not yearn to know its nature in advance and do not hope for its swift arrival. The longer you wait for your reward the more rewarding it will be. This is because you have consistently cut off yourself as its source. This makes a higher source a necessity, a happy and willing necessity from Reality itself.

1696. There is no hope for tomorrow. There is only a reality right now, and this is what you can have.

1697. True bliss is to have absolutely no future at all.

1698. A reminder: You are not here on earth to live up to the expectations of others. You are here to develop into a whole and happy human being.

SIMPLIFY

1699. You have to learn the spiritual art of doing only one thing at a time and doing it thoroughly.

1700. Any kind of work should be done only with the mind, never with feelings.

1701. Don't tolerate disorder.

1702. Classification supplies simplification.

1703. Don't sacrifice accuracy for stupid speed.

1704. Short cuts will drive you nuts.

1705. Keep your mind where your body is.

1706. Yes, we're talking about spiritual things.

POETRY FOR PERSONAL PROGRESS

1707. Stay loyal to what is royal.

1708. Give up and you will go up!

1709. You're sinking with thinking.

1710. To reach the top just be a flop.

1711. Be logical not theological.

1712. Pretense makes no sense.

1713. It is bad to be mad.

1714. The thrill is ill.

1715. Noise has no poise.

1716. Tension steals your attention.

1717. Be curious not furious.

1718. To win the race remain in disgrace.

1719. My constant fakery is no slice of cakery.

1720. The ache is a fake.

1721. Fear can't hear.

1722. There is no fright in the Light.

1723. Grow and you will glow.

BRIGHT REVELATIONS

1724. Seek revelation not comfort.

1725. Truth presented itself to you hundreds of times today. You didn't recognize it because it looks like a stranger to you—and just now it is. It was trying to break through to you with the bright message that everything is dark. It is a cheerful, positive, inspiring message for you to hear that you are bad.

1726. You must see the darkness before the dawn. If you don't first clearly see the darkness you will never experience the dawn.

1727. The next time you leave somewhere to go home, ask yourself what kind of a person you're going home with. If you have an overwhelming feeling of despair and hopelessness—congratulations—for you have spent your life up until now in covering up this fear of ceasing to be, by not knowing that now is your eternity. Oh, you're so fast at covering up that sense of desolation, of inner wilderness. Too bad. Do you have the intelligence to do what you've been told to do? Go through your dark valley so you can get past it.

1728. God will never abandon you once He has taken you to a dark place inside yourself. He will stay there with you until the darkness turns to Light.

1729. If you think first about love, you will end up with hatred. If you think first about hatred, you will end up with love.

1730. Dark revelations lead to bright revelations.

1731. Ask God to qualify you to receive the higher revelations.

BUMPTIONS

1732. What blocks investigation that brings revelation? An assumption not seen as an assumption.

1733. Assumptions cause bumptions.

1734. Surely I must possess one of the miracle-minds of the ages. Listen to this incredible fact. In every dispute I am always right and the other person is always wrong.

1735. The human mind wants to think that the way it presently thinks is the only way to think.

1736. My cowardice and stupidity are clearly evident when I criticize a decision that I did not have to make.

1737. Familiarity is not security.

1738. Get bored with paying attention to nagging thoughts. *This is much deeper than you think.* Just yawn and say, "Ho-hum" to them.

1739. The mind only seeks its own level. This is all it can do.

1740. Your limited thinking limits God's capacity to do for you what He can do.

1741. Watch the river of your mind. Know when you think useless thoughts.

END TORMENT

1742. God is waiting for you to turn to him one-millionth of a second after you do something wrong.

1743. Real correction arrives by turning these facts into personal perception.

1744. You must come to a stop and remain at a stop.

1745. Inner and intense punishment is a harmful vibration that cunningly masquerades as a right and necessary movement.

1746. Practice *abrupt interrupt.*

1747. When tormenting thoughts invade you, I want you to scream with right emotion, "No more torment! No! Absolutely not! 100%!" You get fierce in a new way—not in hostility.

1748. Punishment is not to get the reward of spiritual growth.

1749. Self-interruption is inner construction.

1750. The secret of Heaven is to discontinue myself from moment to moment.

THE SECRET OF SPIRITUAL SUCCESS

1751. All good things come to anyone who refuses to be intimidated by his own despair.

1752. Your despair is your unconscious sensing that up until now, it is all in vain.

1753. Truth allows you to fail without being a failure.

1754. Never try to turn failure into success. Instead, seek to turn failure into understanding.

1755. You can be in defeat without being in despair.

1756. Do not turn against yourself, no matter how badly you may have blundered in the past, for blundering exists only in man-made time and your true nature does not live in time but in the pure present.

1757. The secret of spiritual success is to be utterly discouraged but continue to work.

DON'T THINK ABOUT IT

1758. Do you understand that thoughts pose as people?

1759. The intellect is a tool but it is not you.

1760. You are always thinking about what other people are thinking about you.

1761. I am nothing at all I can think about.

1762. What your usual mind cannot comprehend can be understood instantly and fully by your spiritual nature. This is why so much emphasis is placed on becoming passive to ordinary thought. This mental passivity permits your spiritual nature to become active with its instant insight, which then becomes your own instant insight.

1763. If your relationship with another person is right, you need give no thought about his kind of relationship with you. The sun is always in right relationship with midnight on earth because it really has no relationship with it at all. Darkness can descend on this earth a million times but the sun still knows only its own light.

1764. When you see that you can't think your way out, you will have made a very big breakthrough. God, Reality, Truth is without thought.

WHERE IS THE PROBLEM?

1765. Anytime you meet a challenge or difficulty or problem say, "Time to take the next step up."

1766. To attain the level where you are neither attracted nor repelled by the world and all it contains, know that you are now living from attraction and repulsion, until you no longer know how to appear or what to choose. You forget your spiritual promises to yourself. Only you can keep your promises.

God, Truth, Reality is above all, but you let that petty thieving mind steal what you could have. You have to have more problems so you can use them to grow. Why, you have griefs you've never even met. You want to deny to yourself that you've ever promised yourself to get straightened out. You have—and everyone has—an unseen hysterical shriek inside. Some event could produce this result in you. As long as you have it in you, you're a terrible danger to yourself and to others. This is part of your work, to invite spiritual help to dissolve it. When you lose yourself, there will be no fear of exploding for there will be nobody to explode. Learn that you do not have to fear the shriek, the explosion.

1767. Don't try to solve the problem. Rather, see through yourself.

1768. If you are compelled to think about the condition, it controls you. If you don't need to think about it, you control it. But this kind of control is unique. It is a state in which there is neither a controller nor anything to be controlled. It is non-mental control, something like a man in good health who never needs to think about controlling illness.

1769. You handle a problem perfectly by not being there. When someone throws a hard rock at you and you're not there, how can you get hurt? That is what spiritual success is, not existing to the attack, to the problem, to the fear.

1770. Reality will deliver you from all dangers, now and forever.

1771. Now is problemless.

THE SUPREME CHOICE

1772. Both hell and Heaven start in this life, either hell for eternity or Heaven for eternity. You make your choice here.

1773. Either you let yourself be absorbed by something higher or you will be absorbed by what is lower.

1774. The conscious rejection of evil is the beginning of goodness.

1775. Do right even if you are tempted to do wrong. Do right even if it means losing a friend. Do right even if you fear the consequences. Do right even if you don't want to. Do right even if it frightens you. Do right even if it feels strange. Do right even if it arouses criticism. Do right even if you must go against the entire world.

1776. Anytime you please yourself, you make it harder to get spiritual pleasing.

1777. The reason all can be well right now is because union with Truth is possible right now.

THE WATER OF TRUTH

1778. Give your willingness to let the Truth flow through you.

1779. There is more water in the spiritual oasis than you can possibly drink.

1780. The water of Truth will put out the fires of hell.

1781. Self-teaching consists of letting drops of Truth fall into the inner volcano.

1782. The pool of pure water is waiting for you. But you can't think it into your life. You can only receive it into your life.

1783. Life is never too tough for your higher self, any more than a rock is too much for a river.

INNER-WORK EXERCISES

REFRIGERATOR DOOR   For the next seven days, every time you open the refrigerator door, first know that you are. To be gone from yourself at anytime is wrong.

THERE IS   Watch your mental conversations. Watch your conversation with other people and you will notice how "I" is the most important word in your life. Everything revolves around "I." I am aware you have to use "I" in practical situations such as "I want the car repaired." I am talking about the psychological "I." Effective as of now, you will catch yourself saying "I" in false self-reference and you will say *There.* For example, instead of saying "I am angry," say *"There* is anger."

WHO SAID THAT?   You can begin to catch your false behavior by asking the question, "Who said that?" and you will catch your false personality being pleasant, sarcastic and so on. As often as you can, you will interrupt yourself and say, "Who said that?" And if it is negative in any way at all, that is the invented-self speaking in your name.

EARN THE KEY   Do this exercise which will help you understand the prison you're in and the key to it.

201

You must earn the key. Free yourself from words by making two lists on a piece of paper. Name the left-hand list *Non-religious* or *Psychological Words* and the right-hand list *Religious Words*. Then match pairs of words which have one reality behind them: recovery/salvation, egotism/self-love, Reality/God, delusion/devil, insanity/possession by evil spirits, schizophrenia/hypocrisy, self-defeating behavior/lover of darkness rather than Light, alienated from society/prodigal son, admit wrongness/repentance, understanding/spiritual perception, etc.

When you've written them down, study your lists. Break down the division and find the deeper meaning. This is to help you work against the mechanical part of the mind.

• • •

Chapter 9
THE WAY BACK HOME

WHAT WE WANT MOST

1784. God knows one thing about people, that they are lost and want to come home.

1785. Man believes he is trapped in a corner, never looking up to see the open window above his head.

1786. Look up, and the marvels of God will descend upon you and you will know the way out. You will know what you must do. Look up!

1787. Remove the dark cloud of negative thought and the guiding star of understanding brightly appears.

1788. Never know where you're going. Just know what you want to get rid of.

1789. Think of this one important sentence and reflect on it often: Too much of me is in my life.

1790. There is only one home. That home is yours to find, yours to live in and you don't need a single outside influence or human being to find it. You don't need anyone. Truth is kindly, not cruel. Do you think you would be put here on earth, with the opportunity to find out who you really are and then find nothing but endless obstacles? There can be an end to the journey and you can come back home.

THE MARVELOUS ROAD BACK HOME

1791. You are on the long, hard but marvelous road back home.

1792. To go home you need to know where home is.

And to know where home is, you must first know where it is not.

1793. Let me give you a profound spiritual lesson: If you want to reach North Carolina, you must first leave South Carolina.

1794. The problem is that you insist on finding your own home instead of letting God show you where it is.

1795. Home is not rearranging your thoughts. Home is dropping thought.

1796. The only reason you feel bad is because you and God have nothing in common.

1797. You don't go home because you can't stand the silence.

1798. To have quietness you must give up noise.

1799. You are putting misery in place of contentment.

1800. The next time someone says something that is insulting, why not just sit back and be quiet so that you can understand your nature?

1801. God and your wish for God come together, and they blend.

1802. You will be one of the rare, unique human beings who has succeeded in the task for which he was sent here—to return to God.

FIND YOURSELF NOW

1803. God says you are not lost. It is because you think you are lost that you feel lost.

1804. Anything different from your muddled nature is the *enemy*.

1805. A person's unhappiness is that he doesn't know how to find himself. But a true person's happiness is that he does know.

1806. If you have lost yourself, then think of the pleasure and the relief of finding your wallet or keys you lost somewhere. Think of the pleasure and different kind of human being you are inside when you have recovered a lost object and compare that to the enormity of finding yourself, of finding out who you really are.

1807. Beauty is finding yourself.

1808. When you see there is no self to be lost you are found.

THE COSMIC COMPASS

1809. Now you have to think to keep yourself in place. Wouldn't it be nice just to drop that, the scheming and the planning and the fooling around and changing directions? It does drive you crazy. Drop it.

1810. Stop looking for ways to do things and simply start doing them.

1811. Gradually you less and less interfere with the flow of Light coming down to your mind. And it flows through you constantly, throughout the entire day.

1812. There is a beautiful alternation between practical thought and understanding which happens all by itself. Truth looks down—you are looking down too—and directs you so that there is a natural alternation without you being involved. It can only happen when you are not involved.

1813. If Truth is leading you, it will also make decisions for you. And since these decisions are right, they will also make you feel right. So what does it mean if you are still using your usual mind to make your own strained decisions? It means you are not yet taking your decisions from the available cosmic compass. Remember that Truth will never lead you into a circumstance without also showing you exactly what to do while within it. It is Truth's very nature to reveal clearly to you your needful actions. It is impossible for Truth to abandon you. If you feel abandoned, you should see that you have carelessly led yourself into the circumstance. This insight allows the cosmic compass to correct your life-direction.

EXPLORING OUR INNER GEOGRAPHY

1814. Where are you living mentally?

1815. You are sad only because you are absent from home and since you can return home, sadness can end.

1816. Catch yourself in the secret recesses of your mind.

1817. A sad condition grips you only because you grip it.

1818. There is never a need for you to feel sad over anything.

1819. Whatever depresses you has no real existence.

1820. Gloom is an immoral stage performance.

1821. Sadness is of the devil.

1822. All negativities and sour moods are connected, so that if you get rid of one of them you get rid of all of them.

1823. When sad, we need only realize that we are in the wrong place internally, like a lark that belongs in the sky, not in a cage.

1824. Become an expert in internal geography.

THE CIRCLE OF SELF GOES NOWHERE

1825. Prayer: Please solve my problem but please first show me what it is.

1826. Stop wanting the survival of the false self.

1827. What we invented to be our protector has turned into our tormentor.

1828. You still think you are inferior because you want to be superior.

1829. When you condemn yourself, you confirm yourself.

1830. You want to remain a child but have everyone treat you like an adult.

1831. Your defensiveness is always followed by offensiveness.

1832. The less a man controls himself the more he will be forced to try to control others.

1833. The more cruel a man is, the more he will demand kindness from others.

1834. The less you have on the inside that is real the more you try to make up for it on the outside.

1835. Just say, "There I go again."

1836. Stop protecting the source of your misery, yourself. Thinking about yourself is circular. It will not solve any problems.

SPIRITUAL FREEDOM

1837. Freedom is not the opposite of your usual state, but above it. Liberty is vertical, not horizontal.

1838. My spiritual level consists of my daily internal behavior.

1839. There is a simple test of your mental maturity which is this: You are immature to the extent that you get flustered and annoyed by unexpected events. A mature mind may meet many unexpected events but is not caught unaware by them. Not having a mind frozen with ego-demands for what should happen, he never fights the unexpected and is therefore able to handle it with calm intelligence. His inner resources are far superior to external events. He is like a man who owns a secret farm and who is therefore unconcerned when the grocery market runs out of food.

1840. A description of a free mind: You can never give it more than it can bear.

1841. A free mind is bright and alive.

1842. Inner liberty can be judged by how often a person feels offended, for you can no more insult a mature man than you can paint the air.

1843. Your actual level of spiritual health reveals itself each time you leave practical thought. An unhealthy mind instantly falls downward to self-centered thought such as returning to a grudge or feeling left out. A healthy mind rises upward to levels of inner-development such as reviewing a spiritual lesson or seeing through the falseness of fame. As an example, two men work side by side in a factory giving practical thought to turning out furniture. The noon whistle blows. One man departs from practical thought to scheme how he can take some small advantage of someone. The other man leaves practical thought to ponder how human affairs are dominated by personal craving disguised as noble ambition.

1844. Your mind must surrender to the Spirit. Leave hypocrisy to the spiritual kidders. See how long you can go during today simply alternating between practical thought and spiritual self-watching, which are both good. Don't fall asleep by going into negative thought, loving self-pity. Study and put first the spiritual world. Think of everything in life as belonging either to the visible or the invisible world—and remember, the invisible world precedes and creates the visible world. So why would you ever try to change the physical? When you understand real causality, the last thing you'll be interested in is altering the visible. You'll want to spend as much time as possible in the invisible world.

GOD IS WAITING

1845. You must resolve to take the spiritual journey, no matter what.

1846. The highway to permanent healing and secure existence is well-marked.

1847. The road to Heaven is straight through hell.

1848. Hell is not knowing who you are while you still want to be someone.

1849. You don't really like being you, do you? You just don't know what else to do.

1850. When you are nobody to the world, you are everything God wants you to be.

1851. God is faithful. Let Him be just that to you.

1852. Anytime you want you can walk away from yourself.

1853. You take one step towards God and He'll take two towards you.

WANT TO GROW FASTER?

1854. Here is one way to grow fast. When your feelings scream at you to do the wrong thing and your mind instructs you to do the right thing, obey your mind.

1855. Do what is right even while feeling nervous about it, knowing that doing right for the first time is always accompanied by nervousness on the part of your wrong nature. Let your right action attract its own right feeling, which will always happen by the power of spiritual laws. This is how lasting inner-harmony develops.

1856. Face the enemy instead of running away.

1857. When you see the monster of self-pity say, "No, you are not me and I am not you."

1858. Experiment instead of yield.

1859. Just suppose I don't have to be taken over by that dark feeling of depression. Just suppose there is another way to live.

1860. Aren't you tired of being scared?

1861. Never expect anyone to put you at ease. Just be at ease!

1862. God will back up all true statements you make.

1863. You no longer have a good opinion of me? Hooray! One more trap smashed.

1864. There is something in you that wants to remain dull and unresponsive.

1865. Do it now. Get it done. Bang! Bang! Bang!

1866. The lower world tells you what to *do*. The higher world tells you what to *learn*.

1867. You give up too easily. Go out and try to accomplish something that's very difficult, something that's a thousand-to-one chance of success. And persevere and persevere. The results of your task are not important. What is important is the knowledge you will learn about yourself.

1868. It is better to be a slow learner than a no-learner.

1869. There are certain prayers that receive an instant answer of "yes." Here is one of them: "As usual, I have been hasty and foolish. May I please start all over again?"

1870. You can trick the devil as often as you want.

1871. Escape hell by going to its center.

1872. What is the answer? Total humiliation without resistance.

1873. You are not going to stop until you win, the winning being your complete defeat. Thank heaven!

1874. Avoid nothing. Go through everything.

1875. Get down on your knees and thank God Almighty that Truth exists.

WELCOME TROUBLES

1876. Why do you limit your spiritual growth?

1877. Don't waste the works of the devil. Spiritual roots can grow deeper in adversity. Use the inner, raging storms. Have sight without flight or fight. Remain a seer. Nothing is too much. All storms are for growth. Remember, no exceptions!

1878. From now on you will welcome your troubles with great glee.

1879. You can use every situation to stay awake.

1880. When things are at their worst, you're supposed to be at your best.

1881. Use negative states for learning.

1882. Be of good cheer. Behind every dark cloud are more dark clouds.

1883. Discouraging facts are very encouraging. Why? Because they prevent us from falling into lazy delusions which prevent real inner work.

1884. Why can you be cheerful?—"I am on the way out."

REMEMBER YOUR AIM

1885. Come back to yourself.

1886. I will give you a fundamental truth. Your free nature, your essence, your kingdom within—call it any name you want—is free from all problems, from all anxieties, from all tensions, from all nervousness, from all groping around in the dark as to what life is all about. Your original nature is a totally free element. It has no problems at all. This is Truth. This is Reality. This is what God is—and God cannot have any problems at all. When we are unified with this state, when we have come back home to it, we are free human beings.

1887. There was a contest in hell to see who could come up with the best idea for stopping spiritual students. The demon who won gave this suggestion: Get those who have a chance to break out to forget their aim. Triple the attack on spiritual memory.

1888. The essence of spiritual growth is to remember.

1889. What you have to do is make a mighty effort to remember the bit of sunshine, that different experience. This is what you must do as a counterattack to dark forces. It means this bit of wisdom will stay with you.

1890. There is a higher association, a higher place to live. It's with something that you won't know about until you listen to the teacher, which is Truth itself. Listen to the teacher and understand. Ask God to help you understand. That's all you need.

1891. You have forgotten who you really are. Truth itself will help you to remember.

CHANGE IS ESSENTIAL

1892. When you are afraid to change your inner nature, for heaven's sake, do it anyway!

1893. The fear of change is the cruelest hoax that has ever been played on mankind.

1894. Dear Heaven, help me proceed inwardly, spiritually, no matter how afraid I am to do so.

1895. Consent is all you need to have. God will provide the courage.

1896. The entire secret of spiritual growth is to simply stay with whatever is happening to you without trying to change it.

1897. Nothing changes in time. Things change in the absence of time.

1898. When you spiritually relax, you are putting yourself in a new position. Now don't fear this new feeling!

1899. Real courage consists of departing from the false while not yet knowing what is true.

1900. Be incredibly fierce with darkness, for it must obey the higher impulse to change.

YOU CAN'T PLAY IT SAFE

1901. To play it safe is to play it dangerous. To risk all is to win all.

1902. The only psychological peril is to not understand the peril.

1903. The false self always feels itself in danger. Watch your next move to protect yourself.

1904. Anytime you do or say anything to be safe, you're in danger. Here's a technique to use. Ask yourself, "Am I a problem to myself?" An honest answer would always be *Yes*. Saying *Yes* to this question is still on the level of thought but it is right thinking—it re-directs the flood to the productive power of a higher energy.

1905. You can define and explain cosmic safety to yourself by asking yourself this question, "When I clearly see that a trap is in fact a trap, does it exist as a trap for me?"

1906. I don't learn by doing what I always do. I learn by doing what I can't do.

1907. You keep asking me how to take the terrifying leap into the dark, the noble leap that will carry you through the darkness to the Light on the other side. Here is how: Give up your confidence. Abandon all confidence. You now have various vague confidences and must drop each one. For example, drop the comforting confidence that you will be able to reach the opposite side without sacrificing your memorized nature. Have no confidence in that dismal distortion. Have no confidence when leaping into the dark unknown; otherwise, you are not leaping at all. Leap without confidence in anything and at the very moment you fear doom on the rocks below, you will be held aloft by angels' wings. If you do not know how this miracle can happen, it is not needful to know in advance, for God knows, for He is the miracle-worker who will keep you safe. From the start of your leap to your arrival on the solid ground of the other side, you will be safe even when you do not feel safe. You see, you don't need confidence at all. You need only God.

LONELINESS

1908. Loneliness is an impostor which makes you feel far apart from life but you can see beyond it to happily find yourself approaching home.

1909. No lonely person ever goes home to an empty room. He goes home to an empty head.

1910. Loneliness is caused by trying to find a sense of completion where it can't be found.

1911. In order to advance, deliberately enter into a new kind of loneliness.

1912. Allow yourself to feel 100% lonely. If you will do this and stay with the pain, it will shatter and you will never be lonely again.

1913. Be all alone until you can't bear it anymore and then make yourself more alone. This doesn't mean to go and sit by yourself in your room. It means to be alone right in this room and not be stolen.

1914. When you're really all alone, then you will really know there is no one there to be all alone.

1915. You find out there is no loneliness as long as you are what you're supposed to be, a self-complete human being.

TRUE LOVE

1916. For construction or destruction, you get what you love. Moreover, you are what you love.

1917. The best way to fall out of love is to get close to your love.

1918. You love the world and the world hates you.

1919. Emotion is not devotion.

1920. Cosmic love doesn't give us what we think we want but what we truly need.

1921. Love is indifference to human charm.

1922. You can't find something to cling to, but you can find Something Else that will cling to you.

1923. It is very important for you to know in your heart that God alone loves you.

TAKE IT OR LEAVE IT

1924. Truth seems harsh and negative only to dishonest people, dishonest people who would rather attack than yield.

1925. I want your help only as long as it agrees with my preconceived notions of what that help should be.

1926. A teacher told a student, "I can't do anything more for you because I can't do anything more with you."

1927. I no longer have confidence in you as a spiritual teacher. I have attended five of your lectures and not once have you told me how to victimize people without becoming their victim.

1928. A truthful lecture is boring to an untruthful mind.

1929. It is obvious that he is a very poor spiritual teacher. I have heard ten of his lectures and he is completely incapable of making me understand anything he says.

1930. If you can't understand a spiritual truth, you can at least be decent enough to not make a hostile remark toward it.

1931. When attending your class for the first time, I realized that it was not at all what I expected it to be. Therefore, with my usual logic, I had to firmly conclude that the class was all wrong. My record for being 100% right still stands.

1932. You demand an explanation of certain points in the lecture? That proves that you don't even understand that words cannot explain realities. And you also don't understand the previous sentence.

1933. I dwell in the spiritual palace of pure love and if you deny it, I will hate you.

1934. What you hear in this class is unacceptable to what is injuring you.

1935. I agree heartily with one teaching in this class, which is that this is an insane world. Only a world filled with insanity would fail to recognize my greatness clothed in modesty.

1936. Goodbye, I give you back to the world you have preferred.

1937. This class has no duty to teach the unteachable.

RELIGION AND SPIRITUALITY

1938. Religion is not Godliness.

1939. Because we have forgotten the invisible and true God, we vainly try to make contact by creating visible symbols, which are merely our feeble ideas about God. This explains the human habit of erecting idols and of worshipping other humans.

1940. You can't worship an idol consciously.

1941. All worship involves the weight of thought. The weight of thought causes pressure and pain. You, attached to the pressure and pain, call out to God for deliverance not seeing that the *you* who is the pressure and pain is really your object of worship.

1942. A false messenger cannot deliver a real message.

1943. An experience with man is often taken as an experience with God. An experience with God can never be taken as an experience with man.

1944. Religious leaders are always afraid of losing their false identities which they get through the false identities of their followers.

1945. A sick teacher of religion needs his students to also be sick. In his delusion he takes the weakness and dependency of his students as signs of his strength and authenticity. For example, a sick teacher declares that shyness is a type of modesty, a form of consideration for other people which lets others do the talking.

1946. Listen to these powerful words: God, prayer, meditation, worship, devotion, reverence, humility, sacred, salvation. How powerful are these words, how powerful to conceal the commission of religious crimes.

1947. One cruel trick of a sick teacher is to take a harmful human trait and use clever words to make it appear to be a healthy characteristic. This succeeds in popular lectures and articles because this is what most audiences want to hear.

1948. God talks to and heals the individual. God never talks to organizations or masses of people. What God loves is the individual who wants to learn to love Him.

ON THE ROAD TO WHAT IS REAL

1949. A powerful question: How can you discover the reality beyond fakery unless you dare to venture beyond fakery?

1950. The showcase self is a horrible drain of various types of energy.

1951. Nothing is more tiring than fakery.

1952. The role is the road to ruin.

1953. There is hurt and humiliation in getting caught out of a role only because we foolishly took the role as being real.

1954. You know, no mask can fit so perfectly—the glue can't be that hardened—where we keep it on all the time. You're glad when you can get home and take off your mask and relax and be real for once. Unfortunately, the reality of your state is that of utter exhaustion from having gone through another day in dreadful, burdensome pretense, the pretense of having the answers.

1955. You get involved a hundred times a day in vagrant, unnecessary thoughts, one of which is the false belief that you must be involved in other people's problems. It can be a small difficulty such as not having enough money or a large difficulty such as a serious illness. When someone comes up to you with his problems, you automatically go into the "right" reaction, which could be sympathy, advice, making a decision and so on. You will see that you really resent doing this. The next time it happens, just watch the other person and say to yourself, "What has that to do with me? Why are you crying on my shoulder?" This reaction is very unacceptable to your false self and can be an authentic new experience for you because you are breaking out of the rut of your old habits. Never do anything to keep your image of being nice in place.

1956. There is no way you can be good, so stop trying. Remember the last time you comforted someone or you gave them something? Couldn't you see that there is a part of you that wants to be free of that?

1957. The next time you find yourself in a strange, embarrassing situation, caught out of a role, and you catch yourself saying, "What if people should find me out?" Why don't you find yourself out?

1958. You are living in a truly spiritual world when you have no world to collapse around you.

1959. Say to yourself and to the world, "You go right ahead and see through me all you want. I am not going to hide anymore. I am not going to pretend anymore. I am not going to pretend that I am intelligent, decent, in control and so on. I plead that you see through me as the faker I am." *(Author note: This is about exposing your phoniness, not your private life.)*

1960. By first feeling real, you will then feel pleasant. In fact, they are two descriptions of the same feeling.

PITFALLS ALONG THE PATH

1961. A misunderstanding of spiritual matters always includes a concealed, dark part of us that insists that it does understand. The detection of this self-deception is essential if we are to advance.

1962. Every refusal of Truth has a tricky form of self-glorification in it.

1963. The rejection of Truth supplies a very definite and very destructive false pleasure. This must be recognized and abandoned before the individual can have the true pleasure of accepting Truth.

1964. The old nature increases its attack as you increasingly cease to believe it is valuable.

1965. Before any human being is saved, there comes a critical point. The individual must make the final decision to give up his suffering. If he continues to retain his love of suffering, he will not be saved.

1966. Beware of "progress."

1967. Anyone can succeed if there is still alive in him the plea, "Please keep telling me that I can't win with my present ways. No matter how bitterly or foolishly I fight you, please keep telling me that." As long as this plea remains alive, it will be honored by both the inner and outer teacher. However, if it fades away through carelessness and a lazy yielding to darkness, the seeker's opportunity also fades.

1968. Say to God in your heart that you want to go all the way. This prayer will be heard and you will receive the strength from Heaven to go all the way.

HERE'S HOW TO HAVE MORE ENERGY

1969. Never allow yourself to become psychologically tired.

1970. You must increase your positive energy by withdrawing negative energy.

1971. Be very observant of self-harm in you the moment it occurs.

1972. Instead of feeling bad about being mean, you will say to yourself, "I must go forward." You have then made up your mind to get out of yourself and the total madness. This cuts off the thievery of energy.

1973. Work hard gathering energy when you have no problems.

1974. Your whole day is filled with silly, energy-consuming comments.

1975. Reaction and repetition are a waste of energy.

1976. A word to the gum chewers. You have something better to do with all that energy.

1977. A person who has arrived at the higher place is always assaulted by the enemy who is afraid of losing them and therefore not being able to use them. You see, the whole world is busy keeping on its own level and busy giving its life energy to invisible spirits who live off of it. Evil spirits live off the negative emotions, the wars, the financial panics. These spirits, these evilers, both invisible and visible, live off your energy, your false energy. If you don't give them energy, they will disappear. Now you take that as a personal thing. It isn't going to happen worldwide. I'm talking to you personally.

1978. See what happens when you make no effort either to attract or repel others.

1979. Always exhaust your energy. That is how you get more.

1980. Work fifty times harder than you do.

TRUTH IS OUR ONLY CHANCE

1981. This class is both an invitation and a warning.

1982. There is no sadder state in a human being than one in which a person's pride prevents him from pleading for another chance to find the road home.

1983. God will never abandon any man or woman who still wants Him.

1984. If you reject Truth in favor of your stupidity, then you will have to live with your stupidity for eternity.

1985. Many a human being has lost his way after making a small amount of progress away from the haunted house, because he fell into vanity, thinking that he didn't need God for the rest of the trip.

1986. If someone has only false earthly values and then runs into heavenly values, nothing valuable will happen to him. He will gain nothing because his earthly values neither recognize nor desire the heavenly values in front of him. This means he will go away from the contact as empty as he came to it, while having no notion of either his opportunity or his rejection of it.

But another man who comes into contact with heavenly values and then departs has a definite chance for self-rescue. His vague sensing of his error will bring him back. He is like a hungry man who indifferently picks just one grape while passing through a vineyard and later finds it to be just what he needed.

1987. Your past was foolish but not fatal.

1988. As long as you can feel you're in the wrong place you still have a chance.

1989. Truth never dislikes or rejects anyone who goes away. It just patiently waits for the foolish individual to come back to his senses.

1990. The one who goes away is the one who must come back.

1991. This is the one great opportunity for a man or woman—to come back, to obey the sensing that he acted against himself by departing from heavenly values. To come back is everything.

1992. You have to see that God is your last chance.

GREAT GUIDES FOR RETURNING HOME

1993. Do the Work all day long.

1994. Snap the spell!

1995. Catch yourself in the act of daydreaming.

1996. Stay aloof from yourself.

1997. Don't decide from your intellect.

1998. Put explanation before frustration.

1999. Flee foolish fascination with evil.

2000. Love the Light.

2001. What could you give up to read a little more in spiritual books?

2002. Find some little way to work on yourself.

2003. The first step onto your property—either walking or getting our of your car—is to be a conscious step.

2004. Defy dullness.

2005. Relax, detach, contact.

2006. Deliberately disappear.

2007. Risk all.

2008. No longer live as a winner or as a loser.

2009. Be willing to be a beginner every morning.

2010. When all else fails, try self-honesty.

RELAX FROM YOURSELF

2011. Reflect on this extremely powerful thought. You are the worst thing that has ever happened to you.

2012. You hurt people outside of you because you hurt inside of you.

2013. If other people attacked you physically the same way you attack them mentally, would you still be alive?

2014. Honestly now, wouldn't the world be a nicer place to live in if you didn't live in it?

2015. You can rest in the hands of God or you will remain in the clutches of yourself.

2016. Living from your real nature is the same as doing something worthwhile with your life.

2017. God alone loves you, cares for you and knows how to help you.

2018. Let the Truth be true.

2019. What we are really talking about is a miracle, a miracle that can be yours.

IT CAN BE DONE

2020. The real purpose of life is to leave this life alive.

2021. Follow the voice above the clouds all the way back home.

2022. Darkness is all dark. Lightness is all Light. There is not one speck of darkness in Light and not one ounce of Light in darkness.

2023. It starts out with 1% rightness and 99% wrongness. But that 1% is 100% pure. It is surrounded by all the darkness but it is 100% right. That is the opening through which can flood in your true life. It will come with power, pushing out all the darkness and giving you a new life. When you have the life of God you are happy, for God's life is happy and it is always that way.

2024. The one right part should and must be encouraged and instructed. The wrong parts should and must be rebuked and rejected.

2025. Listen to me. You can do this.

THE FATHER'S HOUSE

2026. We want to get home before dark.

2027. The angels are sending down sparkles from heaven that say, "One day you're not going to have a physical body, a physical life here on this earth."

2028. Our aim is to remember the way back home. Home is there but we must remember the way. Fondly remembering the wilderness blocks remembrance of the way back home.

2029. Say, "I don't belong here." Go slow with this for it contains tremendous power.

2030. All of you have been told how to say, "Stop. I am not going along with you, world, anymore." Whether it is that business world, that fun-time world, you can say, "This is as far as I am going. I am going to wake up."

2031. Put this higher life first. How would it be if you woke up in the morning with the determination to see how far you could go in the next twenty-four hours in growing in the Spirit?

2032. You only have to make it in one way. You have to make it back home to the original kingdom. You have to make it back home to the Father's house.

INNER-WORK EXERCISES

BUILD SPIRITUAL INITIATIVE The next time you see a cat, be aware you saw it. The next time you lift the telephone, be aware you did it. The next time you open the refrigerator door, be aware you did it. The next time you open your car door, be aware you did it. There are numerous small tasks like that which you can give yourself. Make up your own.

SHORT-TERM PROJECTS Make it a practice to give yourself short-term projects. For example, not falling into mechanical behavior such as complaining or trying to impress someone.

CHANGE YOUR NATURE If you do this exercise, your nature will change. For the rest of your life you are never, never again going to dominate ordinary social situations. Let the other person do the talking and you be passive. Just sit back and let the other person blab on and on uninterrupted. Note everything about the conversation, about them and about yourself, like how nervous you get. Then when they ask you a question, notice how your favorite topic of conversation is yourself. There is no condition worse for you than to stay glued to yourself. Unless you get rid of this false personality, the pain will never go.

TURN YOURSELF OFF You must turn yourself off. This means to simply stop the mechanical movement by which you constantly try to find answers. It means you're not going to keep going to the usual sources. Now, don't underestimate this exercise. In the middle of any day, just sit down and watch your mind and see that you can't do anything at all about it. Don't go into reaction over that or leap to a distraction.

Know one thing only: "My mind is madly churning, but I am watching it." If you see the impossibility of saving yourself, you will have learned something; for when you do something for yourself, you become hardened. This exercise will begin to do something for all the questions that hound you. It will show you that there is no point in you continuing to let anyone on the human level answer your questions, including you.

• • •

Chapter 10
TRUENESS IS WAITING FOR YOU

KNOW THIS

2033. The truth about life is that God exists, freedom exists.

2034. You can be the one to take these facts and change.

2035. Those who want to find the secrets of life will always have the capacity to do so.

2036. You have no idea how hard Truth is working to get through to you.

2037. Dark forces want to divert your attention away from your young love of Truth. Don't let them. *Stay awake!*

2038. The only power evil has is your fear of it.

2039. One step beyond where you fear to tread is healing.

2040. Beginning is always the toughest part.

2041. Just know that you don't want to live against yourself anymore.

2042. All you have to do to enter eternity is to deliberately and finally let all thoughts about your survival collapse. Let them go. Don't care for them. Don't put any value on them at all. Don't think that they represent an accurate and self-serving way of thinking because they don't.

2043. Don't complicate it, just do it.

2044. Where you will be 1,000 years from now depends on whether you love and want more of the health you are reading about right now.

2045. The way to make it is to never listen to anyone who tells you you can't.

2046. You are instantly forgiven for having fallen asleep ten minutes ago.

2047. The single most important thing is for you to persist in spite of everything.

2048. If you are one foot outside the Kingdom of Heaven, you are still outside the Kingdom of Heaven.

2049. Keep going in spite of all the obstacles, not knowing what is going to become of you.

2050. More than anything God wants to give you eternal life.

2051. Worth working for? This is the only thing in life worth working for!

2052. What have you done with this incredible gift?

OUR ONLY DUTY

2053. It is your moral duty to be happy.

2054. The truly happy man is one who feels no different when the party ends than he did while it was going on.

2055. The question is, "Why are you working so hard to be happy?"

2056. Happiness is an absence of inner strife.

2057. There is no one there that you have to do a thing for, so stop!

2058. To experience the truly new you must persistently study higher facts.

2059. You have no duty in life but to find God.

2060. Man is like a lost tourist who has forgotten he has a map in his pocket which can direct him to his hotel.

2061. Find yourself, for courage and confidence are as easy as breathing to the person who really knows who he is.

2062. Danger recognized as danger is not hazardous, as with a sailor who sights and steers away from rocks in the sea.

2063. Just as a single wave is powered by the entire ocean, a sincere mind has vast resources at its command.

2064. Like an army doctor treating enemy soldiers, Truth is patient and kindly toward the parts of us which resist correction.

2065. Foolishness is simply the nervous preference for wrong ideas, like a sailor anxiously hugging a broken compass.

2066. It is no more necessary to live at the mercy of mental howls than it is needful to live next door to a zoo.

2067. Inner correction guarantees outer correction just as a repaired clock makes its hands go right.

2068. Your life makes sense when you don't need other people to confirm that it does, which is the true independence of a soaring eagle.

2069. Just as a piano responds to the touch of a musician, a sincere request for solutions will always be answered from a higher source.

2070. We are rewarded according to personal effort, like a man who is given as much land as he can walk over during a day.

2071. Like helpful librarians who aid your search for books, higher powers do for you what you cannot do for yourself.

2072. Healing finally comes to the sincere seeker, like a sick man who awakens in the morning to find himself cured.

REAL STRENGTH

2073. Recognizing the truth is not the same as wanting or living it.

2074. If you want true strength, you must never go to anyone to get it.

2075. When are you going to initiate spiritual action yourself instead of having someone else initiate it for you?

2076. Send up the invitation to God to send down His strength.

2077. The reason you must seek to become strong is because weakness in you is a danger to you.

2078. If you were really as strong as you imagine you are, you would have no thoughts at all about your strength.

2079. Weakness hurts; strength does not.

2080. One of the most spiritual statements you could ever make is, "I've had it." Make it refer to your own weakness of falling asleep when you should stay awake.

2081. Heaven, you give me the strength and I'll give you the credit.

2082. Real strength does not reside in ideas but in a comprehension that is above all ideas.

2083. Self-reliance equals heavenly reliance.

GOD'S WILL BE DONE

2084. Do you really believe that a God who is love—and God *is* love—would want you to continue to live in daily, minutely torment like you do? I'm telling you differently. I'm telling you that you've made a horrible mistake and I'll phrase that mistake. You are afraid of God's love. You love your own darkness instead of God's Light and love. The evidence that you love it is because you live it. You live what you love and love what you live.

2085. Thank God we found out what didn't work and never will. Now, the greatest good news on earth is that there is a way. It's not the way we have tried, but we have to have courage and persistence to stop trying that way. It's incredible that we don't get to the end of our rope before we do. You have to get to the end of your rope, the absolute end of it. If there's another inch there, it's no good. For heaven's sake, get to the end of it and then let go. When you let go of the rope and you stay there, you're beginning to be a human being who can be kindly without effort. You're beginning to be one of the few human beings on earth who ever really became sane. You'll be one of the few human beings who was ever truly *born again.*

2086. Let go and let God reveal to you who you are and what you can be.

2087. What you have to do is simply stop doing what you have been doing.

2088. Suffer the glorious victory of being defeated. And see how you sense you have done something right for the first time.

2089. I can expect right things to happen when I obey God's will and disobey my own.

2090. The glory of God in man is seeing that he is wrong and staying there until a miracle happens.

2091. God's will be done.

IF YOU CAN TAKE IT, YOU WILL MAKE IT

2092. What kind of a person do you really need in your life? That's an easy question. You need someone who doesn't think like you do.

2093. If a man is asleep in his bed and you play sweet violin music he will only go deeper asleep. Get the trumpet.

2094. You are about as awake as Sleeping Beauty and I have doubts about the beauty.

2095. Please tell me something: If I were to describe your actual mental condition as it operates in secret, how would I describe it? Once again, if I were to describe your actual mental condition, how would I describe it?

2096. If I get hostile and aggressive when rebuked, what does that reveal about my actual nature? It also reveals that rebuke was a necessary lesson.

2097. Your unhappiness consists of what you cannot be told about yourself.

2098. How does this describe your inner feeling: *secret scary storm*?

2099. Rebuked people are puzzled and resentful when told they have done something wrong. They try to remember some small little error they have made. Just wait. Just wait until they realize that what they have done wrong is to exist as they do.

2100. There is one admission to yourself that is worth more than attendance at 1,000 classes and the reading of 1,000 books. That admission is, "What an unseeing fool I have been!"

2101. You need never fear the consequences of doing what is right.

2102. If a 100 year-old man saw on his 100th birthday that he had wasted his entire life, at that very moment his life would not have been wasted.

2103. Nothing matters except to wake up.

BE BOLD IN A NEW WAY

2104. If you have not been chosen for self-elevation, you can still choose to be chosen.

2105. Audacious. Never forget it. God loves an audacious human being, someone who will do something beyond his petty little life.

2106. Every time you notice the incredible neurotic boldness of lost people, I want you to match it with your spiritual boldness. Right now in your present false self, you are afraid of nervy people. While you sense there is something wrong with them—that hard, screaming neurotic woman and the demanding man who maybe has authority over you—you are afraid of them. From now on you'll notice their neurotic nerve. And you are going to remember that God is more powerful than that human hyena.

2107. Whenever you are threatened psychologically, silently say, "Do your worst!"

2108. Be so reckless that every day you destroy some small fiend inside of you that's tormenting you.

2109. He dares spiritual things you don't. That's why he gets spiritual things you don't.

2110. How much can I take today?

2111. Where there is a Daniel there are no lions.

2112. Daringly defy darkness.

2113. Refuse to be shut out and Truth has no choice but to open the door and say, "Welcome." Be willing to be no one and let God be all.

RESOLVE TO CHOOSE WHAT IS RIGHT

2114. How long are you going to evade your lack of understanding of the Laws of Life?

2115. The innocence of ignorance is thoroughly guilty.

2116. Anyone who stays outside of the Kingdom of Heaven does so because he wants to and for no other reason.

2117. The Truth is always coming down on this earth, just as a shower of meteors from the heavens showers down on earth. It is exactly like that. But we're unaware of the Truth that is coming down *right now.* Our eyes are turned toward the ground.

2118. A paranoid fearfully imagines that the world is against him, while a man with spiritual insight quietly realizes that the world is against Truth.

2119. If you feel threatened by the devil, you are the devil.

2120. Be willing to give up being bad.

2121. Right attracts right and wrong attracts wrong.

2122. You can refuse to choose wrong even when you don't know what is right.

2123. The right reaction to everything you see in the depths of yourself is no reaction.

2124. I am responsible for realizing that only God has to be responsible for my life.

2125. When you make the decision that you are going to go towards what is right, what is true, stop right there. You have made the decision to be true in preference to people liking you, in preference to wanting things from the world. So far the resolution is pure. You have said you are going to choose what is right. You don't know what is right and you don't have to.

If you refuse to do anything to carry out your resolution to go along the right path, you've begun to separate yourself from the savior in yourself. Don't do what you consider the right and moral thing to do. Then the idea will come into your mind that this is the right thing to do, not because you've convinced yourself but because you've let yourself go.

2126. You don't have a self to be saved. When you understand this, you are saved.

2127. There is no beauty like the beauty of the person who truly wants to know what life is all about.

STOP PUTTING UP WITH IT

2128. You have to allow God to get tough with you.

2129. Away with all those people who let you get away with it.

237

2130. Most human loyalty is simply one man defending another man because they both tell the same lies.

2131. Are you going to spend the rest of your life pleasing a sick world or pleasing God?

2132. When are you going to start to get tough with yourself?

2133. You want mercy from people and you're the last one to extend mercy to yourself.

2134. You are tolerating yourself to destruction.

2135. Don't let yourself get away with it.

2136. Trying to deny these truths is like trying to deny the sun.

2137. There is no torment but self-torment.

2138. Practice self-honesty to where it hurts.

2139. It is bad enough for you to conceal all that hatred inside you without also being a big liar by denying it.

2140. Abandon your desire for the heat of hell and the intensity of your desire for Truth will grow.

2141. Don't you tolerate yourself.

DON'T FEAR THE NUTS

2142. There are two ways to live: the right way and the nutty way.

2143. Use every human relationship to wake up more.

2144. You still believe that the behavior of other people toward you has something to do with you. It doesn't.

2145. Society is like a peanut factory. There's a lot of nuts around.

2146. Don't fear the nuts out in the world or the nuts inside you.

2147. Cut yourself off from nutty people mentally and physically if possible. You cut yourself off from them for your sake, for your life's sake. They don't care about you. They care about using you. And watch what happens when you leave. Watch their childish anger.

2148. Always leave a nut with his own nuttiness. There is your liberty.

2149. I now know that inner freedom means for there to be no wrong connections between me and another person.

WHAT TRUE LOVE IS

2150. If *you* love, you don't.

2151. Love is first of all what you inwardly are and only secondly what you do.

2152. Talking about love does not make a man loving any more than talking about sugar makes him a slice of cake.

2153. Anyone you love according to society's standards of love you really despise.

2154. Possessiveness and dependency are not states of love.

2155. If you can't walk out of a relationship you are exploiting the other person.

2156. When you have found love and love has found you, you need not cling to it.

2157. Love people by leaving them alone. If they want a higher form of love, they will come to you.

2158. Love is the absence of *you.*

ON LOYALTY

2159. If you don't really understand human nature, you also don't really understand politics, economics, religion, marriage, war or any other human activity.

2160. There are two kinds of people in the world— those who are bad and want to be good and those who are bad and want to be badder.

2161. The following is a definite spiritual law: Only when you are truly nice yourself will you attract truly nice people to you. If you have a mere idea that you are nice, you will attract other people who also merely have an idea they are nice and you will deceive and hurt each other.

2162. Other people will like or dislike your company to the degree that you like or dislike your own company.

2163. Some people prolong their unhappiness by dramatizing it, which is like expecting applause for having a headache.

2164. The other person has a right to his own life and you have no right to demand that he give it to your neurosis.

2165. Weakness invites contempt from weak people.

2166. Keep your own personal life private and don't let anyone in, except on the terms you have allowed Reality to set up in you.

2167. You don't have to prove yourself to anyone.

2168. When someone hints that he will turn against you unless you please him, invite him to turn against you at once and with full force.

2169. The bad people are afraid of you.

2170. If you make a physical break with an unwanted person or condition without also making a mental break, you have broken nothing. You are still tied to the other person by a powerful rubber rope that will sooner or later snap you back to the same or a similar condition. Only a mental break, a spiritual break, can free you from a punishing situation. This spirituality can be described as a new and a superior kind of loyalty. You are loyal to your impression of the existence of something higher than anything on earth, including yourself.

2171. Loyalty to an idea is disloyalty to Truth.

2172. Universal Truth is the only power that can ever be loyal to you.

YOU ONLY HAVE TO INVITE GOD

2173. You owe God an apology.

2174. You want God to treat you better than you treat Him.

2175. God cannot care for the parts of you that cannot care for God.

2176. If only you knew how free you are!

2177. Do you love God enough to go against the mob?

2178. You must seek something more important than yourself.

2179. You do not have to know God. You only have to invite God.

LEAVE THIS WORLD BEHIND

2180. God loves a man or woman who stays very close to God.

2181. Heaven is always happy because it has nothing to do with this earth.

2182. The world is gambling but the roulette wheel is rigged.

2183. Nothing this world can do can do anything for this world.

2184. The lives of human beings who do not want Truth are like a spinning top. It spins for awhile and then comes to a stop.

2185. You must see your need for something higher.

2186. There's no way a degenerating man can forget he is degenerating. That is his hell. There's no way a regenerating man can forget he is regenerating. That is his heaven.

2187. If you were truer you would grow faster. You would know that the answer is more work, more work and more work.

2188. Our purpose here on earth is one thing: To find the spiritual cure, to grow, to develop, to rise to the spiritual heights and leave this world behind.

2189. While your body is in this world your spirit will be in another world.

2190. For the rest of today, thank God for existing.

2191. God, help me to not need this world.

THE WAY OUT IS THROUGH

2192. No matter how I presently feel about it, the way out exists.

2193. The guaranteed way to be through with it is to go through with it.

2194. If you see that you love the night, you will not want to be there anymore.

2195. Your inner work is always the same—a sentry watching.

2196. Work for a week to see where we blame other people for our griefs.

2197. There is never anything wrong in permitting yourself to remain insecure. There is always everything right in permitting yourself to feel insecure at all times and in all places. Insecurity is a very beautiful state and it is about time you stopped cheating yourself out of it.

2198. There is no need to be sad about abandoning your whole life. All you have to do is say, "Yes, God, I will do it," and then it's out of your hands.

2199. Remember these three words: Go through it. You must go through the pain so you can come out on the other side.

2200. If you leap, God Himself will catch you.

2201. You have been told the way out.

TRUTH IS EVERYTHING

2202. Truth is knocking on the door of your life endlessly.

2203. Truth is eager to teach you.

2204. Truth is delighted to give us an abundance of rich gifts but our cherished ignorance prevents our reception.

2205. Truth does not think with your mind.

2206. Truth comes through us, not from us.

2207. Truth has its reasons for acting as it does, and every one of them is for your benefit.

2208. Truth is a threat to misery.

2209. Truth tries to influence you to admit you are wrong.

2210. Truth says you can get out.

2211. Truth is more powerful than falsehood. It's no contest if you yield.

2212. Truth patiently waits for us to come to it on its terms, not ours.

2213. Truth can only help an absolutely helpless man.

2214. Truth will show you what to do with yourself every day just as soon as you no longer know what to do.

2215. Truth will never betray you.

2216. Truth is 100% bold.

2217. Truth has absolute authority over anything in this world.

2218. Truth is 100% intelligent. It knows just how to handle spiritual travelers all the way up to the Light.

2219. Truth and goodness can never be stopped.

2220. Truth is eternally compassionate.

2221. Turn toward Truth.

UNDER TRUTH'S DIRECTION

2222. You can live in a house not made with hands.

2223. Permit yourself to be melted down.

2224. Self-absence creates self-presence.

2225. Say this to darkness, "I am not going to suffer because of you."

2226. Put your badness in the open and something higher will take it away.

2227. Deliberately destroy what is making you "secure."

2228. When *you* disappear, all your problems go with it.

2229. Instead of you driving yourself crazy, God can drive you sane.

2230. What an opportunity you have to wake up!

INNOCENCE AND PURITY

2231. Give honor only to that which is pure and noble.

2232. Oh, if you could only see the power of innocence, the absolute authority of innocence over everything in this world.

2233. God has nothing to do with condemning you as a guilty sinner.

2234. You don't know how guilty you make yourself by insisting upon your innocence.

2235. Both self-forgiveness and other-forgiveness occur when the offense is recalled by pure memory which contains no egotistical self. Innocence exists when the imaginary self does not visit memory.

2236. The present moment can wash away all guilt.

2237. There is not one speck of human dust in the Kingdom of Heaven.

2238. Say the word *clearness* ten times a day until the impact of it hits you. Clearness is purity. It is everything.

2239. There is nothing that can stop the purity of what you are hearing.

2240. God is purity. God is graciousness. God is pleasantness. God is everything that your heart wants. Allow yourself to grow into what God wants you to be and you'll find that is what you wanted to be all along.

LET OTHERS KNOW

2241. You are responsible for what you do with what you have heard.

2242. The one kind thing you can do is to live and speak the Truth.

2243. If you take, you will have less. If you give, you will have more. This is spiritual law. The higher kind of giving will be more easily understood by thinking of it as release. You release your old nature, which in turn causes the releasing and the giving of the new nature. In this higher state there is no personal giver and no personal receiver. There is only the natural and healthy giving of the Universe to itself.

2244. As you receive more and more Spiritual Light, there are only two things you will want to do and need to do: 1. Receive more of the spiritual sunshine. 2. Pass it on.

2245. There are people out there who not only need to hear these beautiful truths but they want to hear them. Do everything you can to let other people know about what they're missing. It is all part of your inner growth.

TIME TO GO TO WORK

2246. Oh, what a shame it is that you have no sense of urgency.

2247. It is the unseen that must be seen and you have no time to waste!

2248. You are in pain even when you don't see it.

2249. Most of you have a flippant attitude towards the devil, which means he has won. He exists and torments you because you allow him to.

2250. You and I have no just complaints whatever. All complaints are simply an attempt to keep the laziness going, to sit back and let others do the work. This includes wanting people in class to answer your questions. The easiest thing you can do in this class is to ask a question and let someone else do the work. Your whole day should be spent questioning yourself, your motives as to why you did or didn't do that. The basic principle of these teachings is to question the loves, the hates, the bitterness, etc.

2251. You can refuse entrance to unhappy moods but you must be alert, just as you might close a window at the first sign of rain.

2252. Watch how much attention you waste in nervous glances at nothing. When walking down the street, you see that person with the nice dress and you are lost. It satisfies your idle curiosity. That's what you let capture your attention for a minute or five or so. Watch how anything attractive or repulsive can take you away from yourself. You have your reward. I assure you, there are much better things to do with your life.

2253. The devil wants to prevent you from becoming consciously uncomfortable.

2254. To feel "right," to feel comfortable, is what keeps us asleep. Fill in the blank and see what keeps you asleep: "I will feel right when...."

2255. There are three kinds of people: the workers, the loafers and the saboteurs.

2256. It is time to see that you either want to wake up or you don't.

2257. We are people with work to do and we haven't got time to fool around.

ONCE AND FOR ALL

2258. What is it going to take to wake us up?

2259. Once and for all—what doesn't work, doesn't work.

2260. The lies have never worked and they never will.

2261. You say you have it made? How close is your next breakdown?

2262. You think that I'm brutal with you. I'm brutal with what is brutal to you.

2263. Hell is the refusal to stop lying.

2264. When Robert Louis Stevenson told the story about Dr. Jeykll and Mr. Hyde, he gave more practical psychology than an entire library full of books.

2265. You still cling to the hope you can have Satan and God, Heaven and hell. But you can only have one.

2266. It's your pain or God.

2267. You can have the painful pain or the pleasurable pain. You can have your hostilities and your apologies afterwards, which are phony of course. You can be loved and appreciated and be very popular. But you can't have those and God at the same time. Do you want to have the hard work of getting rid of yourself or live with yourself in hell?

2268. You get what you really want.

2269. God Himself can't make you want to live to learn. That's an interesting point isn't it? If God forced you to devote your life to Him, would that be devotion? That would be tyranny, wouldn't it? And God is not a tyrant. Ah! I know you. I know all of you and I know how what I just said puts terror into you because now *you* are responsible. You are. You are responsible and you'll never ever get away from that fact. Never.

2270. Here is a right prayer: "God help me in spite of myself and this time help me mean it."

A STRONG RESOLVE TO WAKE UP

2271. Human beings are the same everywhere, only in some places the cages haven't been opened yet: crabby, know-it-all, degenerating progressively. So make this your philosophy of life and let it seep all through you: "That may have worked at one time but no more." Really look at her, at him. What does he or she really want? You are now teaching yourself many lessons. Say without words, "What you're saying has no connection with the new me." Now a small spark of light begins to talk for you. "I am really, in a small way, not me anymore." Say this mechanically at first—for after the saying comes the understanding and after the understanding comes the power. And then you'll see yourself walking comfortably all alone through life.

2272. From this day on say, "I am not going to hold my world in place."

2273. I politely decline to fear the wrath or revenge of anyone.

2274. God, please keep alive, energetic and active my wish to be free.

2275. Make a determination to work in spite of everything.

2276. Stop letting others steal your attention. Because you are asleep, you think it's natural and friendly. You don't know how you resent it. Watch where people attempt to steal your attention. You don't want people to steal your money, but you let them steal your psychic energy. Save your energy for the enormous task of waking up.

2277. Nothing can force me to put up with it. And I am talking about the tyranny of my own sickness.

2278. Make the vow that you are not going to go down with the world.

YOUR SPIRITUAL DECLARATION OF INDEPENDENCE

2279. With emotion say, "I am going to do it!"

2280. Here is a truly heroic declaration: "I don't know where I am going, but I definitely know that I am going."

2281. You make up your mind that you are going to do something drastically right with your day. You are going to see your compulsiveness talking and scream with great emotion, *"NO!"*

2282. Declare, "Whatever happens today I am going to use it to see how asleep I am."

2283. You must declare your independence before you live it.

2284. My rights consist of ignoring your idiocy when you scream for your rights.

2285. Declare, "I am no longer going to live a life that is a lie!"

2286. I want to know from myself that God exists. Not from a book, not from the greatest sage that ever existed, but I want to know from myself.

2287. If I have to be the only person on earth to stand on the side of trueness, then I'll do it—because I want it more than anything else.

2288. You are going to have to fight for your deliverance. The rest of your life has to be dedicated to it. You cannot permit anyone to drag you off the path.

THE STARS UP THERE ARE IN YOU

2289. There are higher things to think about.

2290. The help you are about to receive is incredibly wealthy. It is rich because it is coming down from the stars.

2291. If you are the Light, what can touch you?

2292. Everything you need exists right now in God's Kingdom. And when you want to receive it, you will.

2293. Some night you're out and you look up and see the millions of bright twinkling stars up there. And you have a sensing, using a figure of speech, and you say, "How nice to know that my help is up there. My help is coming from the stars." That's good, that's fine. You get a natural picture inside, that's nice.

But now you're tired of being you—how many of you are tired of being you? When you're tired of that, you look up and see the stars. And you get a certain, different kind of a thrill. You'll understand there's something more that you have to do. And here it is very simply. You have to realize that the stars up there *are in you!* The stars up there *are in you!*

Because you have been only *thinking* about stars, instead of going higher than thought and allowing them to come in, you've locked the door to them. You don't see that they glitter. You don't see how high they are, what promise and fulfillment they have to give you.

So you think about that. Now you do think about that. Think about the phrase, "The stars up there are the very same stars that are in me." And they will be twinkling, they will be bright and they will guide you. And they will make the night inside of you bright and cheerful. All because you're willing to give up your concepts of how to achieve personal peace and happiness.

PUT YOUR LIFE IN TRUTH

2294. Don't miss your opportunity to live forever. Don't interpret what I just said with your mind. *You* can't live forever. I have to use words.

2295. You have been given the Truth in many ways. It can be done—and it must be done. Now it is up to you.

2296. The sleeping state is total agony.

2297. Anything, *anything* is worth it to get out.

2298. You are already going through it. You must do so consciously.

2299. God exists. Therefore no excuses are acceptable.

2300. If there were only words to tell you what I am seeing right now. I know the victory is won. It is done. But you are thinking and blocking it.

2301. If you give up your life, God will give you His life.

2302. You aren't going to have any rest until you know from yourself.

2303. Truth says, "Cry out for help. Cry out at once and without hesitation or shame. It is the one chance you have. Sacrifice all your timidities and cry out for help. Your plea may or may not have sincerity in it, but I hear all pleas. If your cry contains even a bit of trueness, I will both hear and answer. If it lacks sincerity, I will hear but will not answer.

"But in either case, you will be helped. With sincerity I will send down angelic impressions which will enlighten your spirit. But if you lack sincerity, I can help you by withholding my help. My withholding will force you to examine your own cry and personally detect its lack of trueness, and knowledge of this can start a development of trueness where none existed before.

"So do your part by appealing to the sky and I will do the rest. I never fail anyone. I know how to handle both the sincere and insincere wish for guidance. I am always ready to show you how to remove yourself from your own weak hands and place yourself in the hands of eternal strength."

INNER-WORK EXERCISES

BE INVISIBLE Try some day to not attract attention to yourself. Try to remain inconspicuous. See how many times and ways you can do it. See how others attract attention to themselves.

TRACK BACK Take one instance of a depressed, forlorn, heavy-spirited state and track it back to its origination point in some thought or comment. Thought-watching is absolutely necessary for you to catch thoughts and comments passing through your mind—false elation, gloom, etc. No matter what you're doing, be a thought-watcher. Watch your thoughts until they dissolve and watch your life and mind become new and fresh.

STUDY THE TRUTHLESS Look at people who have no interest in studying Truth and make a list of their negative qualities. It works every time. Watch their facial expressions, their words, their eyes, what they do or don't do. This is a good mental and spiritual habit which will gradually spread throughout your life.

AWARENESS If we only knew how much others are secretly suffering, we would be very consciously tender to them. If you could only feel this secret feeling, you would treat them differently than you now do. Man cannot feel others because he is asleep.

As you start to wake up, you feel people. You feel their negative feelings which is their secret suffering. People in life do not feel each other. They just feel their own feelings. So you must be wide awake, alert and aware at all times. Be aware while working, eating or whatever of every person who passes by, walks in the room or is in the room. Do not be so self-absorbed in your food or own feelings that you forget your surroundings, like a car passing by or a person or noise, and know that you are in the room.

In a group, feel the feelings of others, otherwise you will think it is your own feelings that you are feeling. Be aware of others in the room. One person might be suffering from sentimentality and you know that. It is a fact outside of you and you might be able to help that person, without him or her knowing that you are the helper!

Practice this all the time. One person in a group of six or ten can keep the sanity *up* instead of down, if he or she practices this awareness.

• • •

INVITATION

Please send us the names and addresses of friends who may be interested in these helpful teachings. We will send them a free catalog.

If you would like several free catalogs to give out to friends, just call or write:

NEW LIFE FOUNDATION
PO BOX 2230
PINE, ARIZONA 85544

(928) 476-3224
Web: www.anewlife.org
E-mail: info@anewlife.org

ABOUT VERNON HOWARD

Vernon Howard broke through to another world. He saw through the illusion of suffering and fear and loneliness. From 1965 until his death in 1992 he wrote books and conducted classes which reflect a degree of skill and understanding that may be unsurpassed in modern history. Tape recordings of many of his class talks are available.

Today more than 7 million readers worldwide enjoy his exceptionally clear and inspiring presentations of the great truths of the ages. His books are widely used by doctors, psychiatrists, psychologists, counselors, clergymen, educators and people from all walks of life. All his teachings center around the one grand theme: *"There is a way out of the human problem and anyone can find it."*

ABOUT NEW LIFE FOUNDATION

New Life is a nonprofit organization founded by Vernon Howard in the 1970's for the distribution and dissemination of his teachings. It is for anyone who has run out of his own answers and has said to himself, "There has to be something else." These teachings *are* the something else. All are encouraged to explore and apply these profound truths—*they work!*

The Foundation's headquarters are located in central Arizona. Classes are conducted on a regular basis throughout Arizona and in Southern California. They are an island of sanity in a confused world. The atmosphere is friendly, light and uplifting. Don't miss the opportunity to attend your first New Life class. For details on books, tapes and classes write: New Life Foundation, PO Box 2230, Pine AZ 85544.